D1613296

THE KING IN
HIS COUNTRY

AT BALMORAL

THE KING IN
HIS COUNTRY

Aubrey Buxton

LONGMANS, GREEN AND CO
LONDON · NEW YORK · TORONTO

LONGMANS, GREEN AND CO LTD
6 & 7 CLIFFORD STREET LONDON W 1
BOSTON HOUSE STRAND STREET CAPE TOWN
531 LITTLE COLLINS STREET MELBOURNE

LONGMANS, GREEN AND CO INC
55 FIFTH AVENUE NEW YORK 3

LONGMANS, GREEN AND CO
20 CRANFIELD ROAD TORONTO 16

ORIENT LONGMANS LTD
CALCUTTA BOMBAY MADRAS
DELHI VIJAYAWADA DACCA

First Published 1955

Made and printed in Great Britain by
William Clowes and Sons, Limited, London and Beccles

ACKNOWLEDGMENTS

This book could not have been written without reference to the King's private records, and without much help and advice. I wish therefore to express my sincere and humble appreciation of the gracious interest shown by Her Majesty the Queen, and to emphasise that the book could never have reached maturity without the continuous help and encouragement from the outset of Her Majesty Queen Elizabeth the Queen Mother.

An important part of the text is the delightful contribution on Balmoral. The author demands anonymity, but in my view this happy passage, provided by a lifelong friend of the King, is a cornerstone of the story.

There are many others, particularly among the King's Norfolk companions, who have helped by recalling events of bygone days, and I am much in debt for their generous response.

Lastly the illustrations, which are a major feature of the book, were taken informally by friends of the King, in the settings which I have tried to describe. I am profoundly grateful to them for making their photographs available.

A.B.

CONTENTS

		Page
I	A New Era	1
II	The Game Book's Story	12
III	Rough Shooting	28
IV	Flighting	39
V	Duck Shooting at Sandringham	53
VI	Summer Holiday	69
VII	The King as a Guest	83
VIII	Broadland Adventures	100
IX	Unusual Occasions	116
X	The Last Season	132
Index to Names Entered in the Game Book		141

PLATES

At Balmoral   *frontispiece*

                                              facing page
"My First Day's Shooting"   6

Balmoral   7

Balmoral   22

Luncheon Interlude   23

Royal Wildflower
Wolferton Splash   54

Ranworth Flood
Frankfort Pond   55

The King in the Highlands   70

Loch Muick
Balmoral   71

Holkham   86

Sandringham   87

Windsor   102

Hickling   103

Balmoral   136

ix

I

A NEW ERA

THIS story starts in Norfolk, and nearly half a century later it ends there. It is, in fact, very largely a Norfolk story, for although the subject of the book is a King of many lands, nevertheless every man must have his home, and home to King George the Sixth was Sandringham. Born at York Cottage, he was very proud of being a Norfolkman, and for him, whenever the royal train rumbled across fenland towards the Wash and Wolferton, he was 'going home'. Towards the end of his life, after his serious operation which hushed the world, he returned at last to Sandringham and wrote to a friend, 'I am so pleased to be back in Norfolk once more.'

This deep attachment was a family inheritance, and both the King's father and grandfather before him had enjoyed the same affection for Sandringham. This demesne as it came into existence at the end of the last century was the conception of King Edward himself. He devised it as a place where his friends could enjoy his hospitality, and he established it as a great sporting centre for their entertainment. In this setting King George the Fifth was brought up, and his spiritual roots were therefore firmly entrenched in its soil.

'For him Sandringham, and the Sandringham ways of life, represented the ideal of human felicity. "Dear old Sandringham," he called it, "the place I love better than anywhere in the world." Here he could recapture the associations of boyhood: recalling the edge of the warren where he had shot his first rabbit . . . Compared to York Cottage, all the palaces and castles of the earth meant little more to him than a sequence of official residences.'[1]

It is hardly surprising that in turn the son of King George the Fifth grew up with the same love for his home. Not only did it

[1] Harold Nicolson, *King George V*.

appeal to him for its early associations and family background, but being a countryman at heart, his main interests and recreation were in harmony with the life of its community. This particular area afforded him opportunities for the pleasures in life which he most enjoyed, the companionship of his family and friends in a setting of sport and seclusion.

'Royal sport' tends to suggest a picture of formal grandeur and elaborate stage-management, and during earlier reigns this conception would have been a fair one at Sandringham. Certainly it was against such a background that His late Majesty was brought up, and a glimpse into the shooting routine of bygone days may help us to fix the point from which he began his shooting career.

When Sandringham was bought by King Edward, high pheasants were not fashionable and any planting which was subsequently undertaken was done without regard for the aerial course a bird would follow after being ejected from the covert's edge. Indeed King Edward was openly opposed to any manoeuvre which might result in elevating the pheasants, since this in turn might have tended to depress the bag. One familiar with the Sandringham sport for many years wrote: 'The coverts which he planted were designed with no intention of producing pheasants which could possibly fly either high or fast, and it was only a few years ago that a monument to the practices of the past disappeared, when Dersingham Wood was replanted. It consisted of a dense semicircular thicket of broom, snowberry, privets and the like, around which were planted at intervals wide screens of clipped evergreens about seven feet high.

'Behind these lurked complacently guns and loaders, some of them perhaps only just more mobile than the pheasants from which they were hidden.'

Shooting was taken more seriously in the next reign, for King George the Fifth was not only a fine shot but a genuine enthusiast, as opposed to the casual performer who regards a day's shooting as simply another feature of the sporting calendar, like a day's racing or a round of golf. At the same time His Majesty was a great traditionalist and was disinclined to reform the Sandringham drill in the coverts. Thus the late King as a boy was first introduced to shooting in its most rigid form, and was never encouraged to prowl on his own over the vast wilds of Sandringham, from the wooded and bracken-covered uplands down to the sea-wall and the Wash. What a chance there was here to learn the game from the bottom! But the opportunity never came his way, nor was the idea put into his mind, for at that time a fundamental knowledge and understanding of the quarry was not considered an essential prerequisite of a sportsman. A man was judged largely by his prowess at driven birds, and, as we have all learned, it is easier to gain distinction when concentrating for many days on one type of shooting than when one's opportunities comprise a good mixture of all forms of pursuit. For the latter, individual and hard-won experience is essential. But after only six small days walking up rabbits with his father and the Prince of Wales, the late King was inserted at the tender age of thirteen into a line of distinguished pheasant shots, and for a number of years thereafter it was only this form of opportunity which presented itself. Leave from the Royal Navy reduced such days to a minimum.

But let us revert to the beginning.

On the evening of December 23rd, 1907, Prince Albert, aged twelve, sat down at Sandringham and made an entry in a new game book. Following details of the bag he wrote, 'My first day's shooting.' He had been using a single-barrelled muzzle-loader, with which his father, grandfather and great-uncle had also started shooting, and after giving this information he noted: 'I shot three rabbits.' The muzzle-loader, a delightful little piece, is still preserved in the Sandringham Estate office, to be used perhaps before long by Prince Charles.

December 23rd, 1907 SANDRINGHAM *Wolferton Warren*

  1 pheasant   Papa, David and myself
 47 rabbits
 —
                   My first day's shooting. I used a single barrel muzzle
 48   loader with which Grandpapa, Uncle Eddy and Papa all
 —   started shooting. I shot 3 rabbits.

On that day a future sovereign indulged for the first time in a pastime which was to become his abiding hobby for forty-five years.

But this day in sporting history had yet greater significance than that, for it was also the beginning of an era. During the decades which followed the whole pattern of shooting was to become subject to radical change, and the rigid formality of the pre-arranged shoot was to disappear. Two or even three sets of beaters were to give place in time to perhaps half a dozen men, and hand-reared birds, after the Second World War, were to become an exception. Large estates splintered into small shoots, the syndicate was born, and many sportsmen, whose forebears habitually shot with a pair of guns, were to become content with a hunt up the hedgerows. A new interest emerged in pigeons and wildfowl, in the odd cock pheasant and vermin. Not only had Dersingham Wood become an anachronism, but the whole attitude to game shooting as it had formerly existed was itself to become a museum piece.

It is impossible to feel that this has been a change for the worse. The colourful pageant of the great days may be something to lament, but it is doubtful if many would derive the same pleasure from it to-day. Nobody believes the man who says he does not like a big bag, for we all enjoy the exhilaration of rapid fire. As the King himself remarked, after killing a hundred head during a coot drive on the Broads, 'It's rather nice to fire one's gun.' But it is a question of how often and in what manner big bags are achieved. The true sportsman would not be content to-day to be committed to his shooting-stick for a whole season, and never to see his guns except when his loader meets him at the first stand. The fortunate, after two or three days' driving of game, are usually in the mood to stand by a flight pool or to set out on an informal maraud. Most of us prefer wild as opposed to reared pheasants, and the highlights we recall at the end of the day are the sporting and difficult shots or the unusual incidents, rather than the totals which we have secured. To all normal shots a heavy bag of easy pheasants is distasteful.

One reason for this is that present circumstances demand a deeper knowledge and interest, and this perhaps promotes a healthier respect for the bird. We cannot be spoon-fed any longer by the agent or the keepers, nor, if we have any knowledge, are we prepared to be. We would prefer to think it all out for ourselves, and either to exercise a close supervision over the proceedings or actually to perform the manoeuvre ourselves. If things go wrong to-day the misjudgment is usually the host's, and it would not be appropriate to abuse the keeper.

Thus the modern sportsman may become once more the *chasseur* of earlier times. The clock-hand has turned almost the full circle, and the keen and accomplished shot of to-day has more in common with Colonel Peter Hawker than had his great grandfather.

The truth is that a softer period was induced by the new comforts of the Edwardian era. The ease of travel and the speed of movement, artificial heating, the possibility of presenting a profusion of game by hand-rearing and other innovations, seems to have taken the stuffing out of most well-to-do sportsmen, particularly of the younger generation of the period. With the loss of their hardiness they lost as well their fieldcraft and sense of sport. This process was regretted by the few remaining experts of the time, and referring to the new trends Lord Ripon wrote:

'With these improvements came an increase of luxury in the conditions of shooting, and sometimes when I am sitting in a tent taking part in a lengthy luncheon of many courses, served by a host of retainers, my memory carries me back to a time many years ago when we worked harder for our sport, and when, seated under a hedge, our midday meal consisted of a sandwich, cut by ourselves at the breakfast table in the morning, which we washed down by a pull from a flask; and I am inclined to think those were better and healthier days. Certainly the young men were keener sportsmen.'[1]

This easy pattern of sport flourished in the early part of the present century, and it took two world wars to kill it. Only when

[1] Watson, *King Edward VII as a Sportsman*.

the rearing of game became impossible, and when there were in-sufficient keepers and beaters to maintain the big shoots, did the sportsman at all levels have to give a hand and get to grips him-self with his quarry. Though to-day in a few centres the scale of earlier days may in some measure have been restored, nevertheless most individuals have learned in the meanwhile many lessons and acquired a better sense of proportion.

There are still many men who frequently enjoy the oppor-tunity to shoot with two guns, but the new trend of thought and approach to shooting among all true sportsmen is there, whatever their opportunity, and the owner of extensive shooting has a far greater need of knowledge and experience, if he is to devise a good plan himself, than the casual walker-up.

Of all persons one might suspect that this new refinement and comprehension would not readily be acquired by kings. Circum-stances, it would seem, would be against it. Yet of all men it was never more true than of His Majesty King George the Sixth, de-spite the unpromising start to his sporting life which has already been described. No more accomplished expert, no man with a more sensitive understanding of his quarry, has trodden the hill and bog of Scotland, or the broad acres and marshes of East Anglia.

It is household knowledge that King George the Fifth was one of the finest shots in the country. But it is equally true that his sporting days conformed to a standard procedure—grouse driv-ing in August, stalking in September, driven partridges in October, covert shoots in the winter, and so on. All good days, days we should all relish.

But there were no 'in-betweens', and there was little variety. This was the pattern of the times, and His Majesty was at the apex of the shooting composition of his reign.

The late King started at the apex, and remained there. For whilst the whole composition changed, he changed with it. In many ways he was foremost in the revolution. And this came about not through his early experience of deafening barrages, but because after he had grown up he decided, so to speak, to go

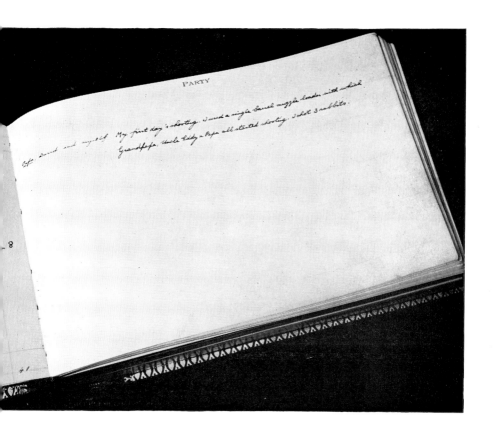

"MY FIRST DAY'S SHOOTING"

*The first entry in the King's game book
made in 1907*

BALMORAL

back to school and to learn the job properly. And later in life when he was drawn to a Scottish estate rich in sporting possibilities, but which was neither royal nor run on such formal lines, he learned to shoot, as opposed simply to firing his gun, all over again.

It would be natural for many to suppose that a man who could arrange a good day's shooting at grouse, partridges or pheasants whenever he had a free day would be inclined to make that choice, and not to seek uncertain chances at more elusive game. This was not the King's way, however, any more than it would be the way of a gifted climber to spend all his days on one easy mountain. The King acquired a fundamental knowledge of all aspects of sport, based on wide experience, and because of the chances he took and the opportunities which he tried there were failures as well as successes, disappointments as well as agreeable surprises.

His interest in country pursuits and the quality of his participation in them were something more than the ordinary outcome of inheritance. By tradition sport in Britain has always been favoured by royal patronage, and in one of its many fields the crown has usually been closely involved. But for a great many generations the sovereign had, according to taste or contemporary custom, been little more than an enthusiastic observer of race or contest, whether the performers were horses, pugilists or fighting cocks; later, as we have seen, when shooting became a fashionable form of entertainment around every castle and manor in the kingdom, kings expected to be confronted with a profusion of carefully manoeuvred game. But without the precision of manoeuvre the royal enthusiasm might well have evaporated, and a pronounced

---

January 5th, 1909 SANDRINGHAM   *Frankfort*
3 pheasants   David and myself
1 hare
9 various   I shot my first pheasant.

___

13

shortage of birds might perhaps have induced a prompt demand for clay-pigeons.

But now, in George the Sixth, we had a new sort of sporting monarch—a king who was not just an observer, nor a casual participant, but who was himself a significant factor in the recreation he so greatly enjoyed. In due time he became, as it were, the author, the producer, the stage manager, and the leading man all at once. Every detail of the royal shooting during his holidays, on however elaborate or humble a scale, was the product of his own thought and contemplation, and as every little phase might develop during the day his concentration, thought, and study were self-evident. Nothing escaped him.

The King's deep love for his land sprang from the sturdy Norfolk roots in his character. Simplicity and truth are the ancient symbols of honest countrymen, and it was these aspects which determined the nature of his well-earned leisure. In his high calling, and later life of exacting duty, it was to the simplicity of life in the countryside that he turned for peace and rest. He longed, certainly, for his shooting, but even this was in reality only the bridge-head to that broader setting wherein lay his true *métier*, in the world of landlord and farmer, of men of plough, scythe and axe, of gardeners and foresters, keepers and ghillies. Among these people he was no remote monarch, but the master and friend. With them he was able, as it was said of another English king nearly three hundred years before, to 'put off the King'. Here he would often go down and visit old pensioners in their cottages and have a yarn; a long line of beaters, either on his own ground or even on that of his friends, was no impersonal squad of ex-

---

January 5th, 1910	SANDRINGHAM *Massingham Belt* and *Grimston Carr*
312 pheasants	Papa, Uncle Alge, Sir William ffolkes, Mr. George
36 hares	Brereton, Sir Charles Cust and myself
3 rabbits	
1 woodcock	
——	My first day with a party.
352	

pressionless faces to him, but real people whose jests and wit he understood and shared. He remembered their names and after a drive would fall into conversation with those who appeared nearest through the hedgerow, and with his remarkable memory invariably recalled some interlude or topic of conversation, or more frequently a joke, which all had enjoyed the season before. One notorious character of russet complexion and impressive moustache he nicknamed after a popular comedian.

Whatever profound differences there may have been in character and temperament, in the times in which they lived and in the state of the nation, it is interesting to note how much George the Sixth and Charles the Second would have had in common out of doors. They both loved the ordinary folk among their subjects and to fall into conversation with them. Of Charles we read, 'In this park,[1] the resort of all the world, he was wont to take that bewitching kind of pleasure called sauntering and talking without any constraint. . . . Here he might be seen of a morning before lunch . . . "With a great crowd of his idle people about him, and here he would listen to all comers".'[2] If crowds were less to King George's liking, he would certainly listen to all comers and interrogate them thoroughly until he had learned what he wanted. Both kings were great gardeners, and devised memorable landscapes of fine shrubs and trees; both were naturalists and energetic sportsmen; but one common interest would almost certainly have engaged them, had they met, from the very outset, a bond which they have shared with no other sovereign in our history. For they both possessed a keen and specialised interest in wildfowl.

[1] St. James's Park.   [2] Arthur Bryant, *King Charles II.*

August 14th, 1911 BALMORAL *Cooper's Well*

1 hare	John Bigge, Abercrombie, young Arthur Grant and
1 rabbit	myself
24 grouse	
—	I shot my first grouse.
26	

For the delights of St. James's Park, and for the confiding habits there of mallard and teal, of pochard and tufted duck, we are indebted to Charles, for he was to this glorious park what Peter Scott is to the Severn Wildfowl Trust. 'A year later all the world came to see the King's brave improvements and the birds with which he was stocking his lake. These ranged from the little ducks he used to feed to that "melancholy waterfowl, between a stork and a swan" brought by a Russian ambassador from the wastes of Astrakan.'[1] Those were the days! What a heartening development it would have been had Mr. Molotov arrived with a gift for His Majesty of a waterfowl, however melancholy, which was a cross between a Siberian crane and a corncrake.

Of Charles again we read, 'The King, who loved all animals, made his park a home for them. Evelyn thought it a strange and wonderful thing to see the wildfowl breeding so near a great city.'[2] From his headquarters at Newmarket or Euston, the Fens and Broadland were temptingly close for his hawks, and Charles, like King George, must surely have gazed often across the glinting silver shallows in the vicinity of the Wash, Ranworth and Hickling and thrilled at the sight of packed companies of duck, coot and swan. The one a naturalist scientist, the other a sportsman naturalist, these two kings were both wildfowlers, only differing in their weapons and methods of approach. Of energy and enthusiasm there was little to choose between them.

Being a wildfowler, His late Majesty's approach to shooting was not conditioned therefore by any prodigious opportunities which may have been available, nor is this ever the case with good sportsmen. One cricketer may have a fine playing-field in his private parkland, whilst his neighbour may have nothing but his kit, but that does not render the zeal and application of the first less refined than that of the second. So in the case of true sportsmen the artistry and comprehension of great shots does not differ because of their varying fortunes in the material sense. Wildfowling 'is a healthy and interesting pursuit, and one in which a little success gives much content; for the pleasures of fowling are

[1] Arthur Bryant, *King Charles II*.   [2] *Ibid.*

in no degree relative to the numbers slain, as three or four ducks
killed, after a deal of thought and trouble, may easily give you
greater satisfaction than, perhaps, thrice this number obtained
without any difficulties.'[1]

His Majesty was as happy waiting for pigeons on a winter's
afternoon as any of his subjects. He was as sensitive to the
fascination of a marshland flight as any good wildfowler. And his
game book reveals that rough days in Scotland, January days at
Sandringham, adventures afloat in Broadland were as diverting to
him as the more prolific engagements of standard pattern. He
thought and spoke the same language as the wildfowler, the
keeper, the sporting parson, the small farmer, the rabbit-trapper,
and the rest of us. In this respect he was 'plus royale que le roi'.

This is a humble account of a few of His Majesty's experiences
with a gun. But it is just as much a glimpse into the story of an
ordinary sportsman of humility and accomplishment.

[1] Sir R. Payne-Gallwey, *Letters to Young Shooters.*

September 1st, 1911 BALMORAL   *Micras Moors*

33 partridges   John Bigge, Edgey Knollys, Mr. Jones, McNab and myself
 4 rabbits
 3 black game   I shot my first partridge.
 6 grouse
──
46
──

II

THE GAME BOOK'S STORY

When a man is no further versed in shooting than just to
have become quite expert at bringing down his bird, I conceive that he has only learnt about one-third of his art as a
shooting sportsman.

PETER HAWKER, 1814

WHEN, with due reverence, you turn the crisp pages of His
Majesty's beautifully kept game book, it is at once apparent that
he belonged to that minority among the shooting fraternity
whose keenness and enthusiasm are characterised by an almost
professional thoroughness in the practice of the sport. To those
who endeavour to embrace the other two-thirds referred to above,
the pursuit becomes an art, not only in the handling of the gun and
actual marksmanship, but in the approach to and manoeuvring
of the quarry. A customary feature in the lives of such people is
the maintenance of careful records down to the smallest detail.

For the enthusiast an unrecorded day is incomplete. It is not
enough to remember only the general scene, and the sun and the
wind, and that the party had killed about a hundred head. Such
memories must fade, and in a few years one might remember only
the name of the place. A game book, however, permits one to live
experiences all over again; 'when, perhaps, rheumatism and old
age prevent the fowler from following the ducks and geese on
marsh or tide, his delight will be to revel in reminiscences of bygone times, and shoot his birds over again by the fireside, with,
maybe, the roar of the wind in the chimney as a reminder of many
a wild night or day passed ashore and afloat.' More particularly
records enable one to recall how each season has varied, how a
shoot improves or otherwise, and to benefit by the experiences of
the past. These aspects were of great interest to His Majesty.

Game books, to shooting men, are volumes of perennial fascination, and the books of shooting strangers are sometimes especially revealing. At the outset one may be no wiser than that the author is out regularly with a gun, but after perusal of his game book he at once comes into focus; your portrait of him, hitherto in monotone, is now rich in colour. How strangely your estimation of him is enhanced when you discover that he waits for pigeons in the snow, or that there are regular entries of expeditions before dawn in order to be on a marsh before flight. These events in themselves are not exceptional, it is their constant repetition which is significant. Many a man has been dragged out in the early darkness, and having returned cold and empty-handed, is ready with prompt excuses on the next occasion. But the man who makes a habit of it cannot, because of the perversity of wildfowl and weather, be seriously concerned about the bag. Thus a game book permits the reader to classify a man as a true rough shooter and huntsman, or as simply a casual participant in conventional expeditions.

All know that His Majesty was a keen shot, but the imagination on that advice alone can hardly devise anything more original than a picture of beaters and pheasants, of cheerful family parties in winter woodland, or of grouse driving and sunny picnics in

---

August 29th, 1925 GLAMIS *White Top* and *The Warren*

		Michael and David Lyon and myself
1	hare	
11	rabbits	
1	woodcock	
1	snipe	Fine but very windy. Very few duck and teal in.
4	wild duck	
7	teal	
3	pigeons	
1	black game	
18	grouse	
1	capercailzie	
2	various	

50

the heather—happy scenes all of them, but of the central figure
there is conveyed very little. Although we know that His Majesty
was abreast of the times, it is difficult without evidence to dispel
entirely from the mind that well-established impression created
by faded photographs of fifty years ago or more, of portly
groups surrounding His Majesty King Edward, of beards
and gaiters, of tweed capes, stiff-collared head keepers, and a
strange assortment of headgear. This tableau is probably the
popular interpretation of 'royal shooting'. And so, knowing only
that His late Majesty was a countryman of profound and simple
understanding, it is difficult to assemble the correct composition
of his sport in the mind. But his game book clarifies all these
problems for us.

There are countless observations written in the book by His
Majesty which would serve our purpose, but one is enough to dispel any mist and to reveal him in sharp outline. This single entry
is sufficient to indicate what 'royal shooting' for King George the
Sixth might comprise. On a January evening before the war he
wrote: 'Snow and very cold east wind. I spent four hours in a hide
in a kale field.'

Now there we have it, a true measure of the King's enthusiasm
and experience. Not since King Charles himself had an English
sovereign shown such determination in the personal and indi-
vidualistic opportunities of sport. But here was a king who, although there were pheasants in quantity available and men to
drive them, preferred to go out in an easterly blizzard and squat
in a kale field.

The personal game book notes written by His Majesty in his

October 12th, 1925   ORMISTON   *Windy Mains*
  28 pheasants   Sidney Elphinstone, Walter Dalkeith, Dick Molyneux,
434 partridges   Ivan Cobbold, Jock Lyon and myself
  80 hares
   4 rabbits

---

546   Plenty of birds and perfect day. They flew very well.

own hand are certainly brief, but they tell more than mere figures, and a book only of quotations could have provided the reader with some sort of estimation of the King's rightful place in the shooting world. This was by no means confined to grouse butts, or 'stands' beside covert and hedgerow, and only a handful of sportsmen and wildfowlers to-day could equal the prowess and experience of the King himself. In that kale field he shot 43 pigeons from his hide, and undaunted by wind and weather he was ready for more next day. There is, however, a hint of relief in the note of the next evening, 'Not many pigeons came in. I was in a warm wood for a change.' 'Warm' may not be an epithet which would have commanded universal acceptance.

Elsewhere there are regular references to duck flighting, to woodcock, rabbits and snipe, which testify that this true rough shooter was not primarily concerned about the size of the bag. The charm of solitude, the fascination of marshland awakening, the changing pattern of the sky, the other birds seen which you do not shoot—all these things lure the sportsman who is a country-man or naturalist as well, and prompt the high anticipation with which he goes to bed the night before. It is a question of what is felt and seen, as much as of what is brought home.

Such a man must surely derive more, then, from the ordinary day driving or walking up game. Between spasms of shooting the day is packed with interest. The sky is seldom empty, a woodland never lifeless. Because of his understanding and knowledge this man is always alert, anticipating, looking in the most likely places, or pausing to watch some small interlude of the wild. To be in the country is his first objective, to bag the game by ingenuity and

---

August 12th, 1927 Glamis *Muir of Balgownie*
2 rabbits   Michael and David Lyon and myself
2 woodcock
6 grouse   We were out for two hours. Had to get a grouse for dinner.
1 various

—

11
—

understanding the next. All this you can discover from a game book, and the game book of King George is packed with such vivid and colourful testimony.

His Majesty's passion for care and accuracy dominated all aspects of his life and the records of his favourite recreation were certainly not spared this discipline. Many of us keep game books most conscientiously, and intend to record, as he did, every detail of every bag. Yet there must be very few who have not missed something, unintentionally, during a shooting life. By chance it may not have been possible to secure the bag; after a rough day a host may not have bothered to differentiate between some allied species, and sometimes we are not informed of the next day's findings by the keeper. In the King's book, however, no detail is missing; every season is added up in total, every figure cross-checked, and statistically, one can harbour no doubt, this is a record as complete as it is accurate.

His Majesty's insistence on extreme accuracy was keenly understood by his staff. The game card was sent in to him during the evening after shooting and the slightest mistake, either in the description of the bag or in the list of the guns, would attract his attention at once and the necessary alteration would be made.

To the connoisseur of shooting records one of the most agreeable features of the royal game book is its neatness. Perhaps it may not always be our own fault if our game books look untidy, for standard books which may be bought in a shop are often aggravating and archaic in their layout. For the average shot the few available patterns and game lists are far removed from reality and practical requirements. How often, for example, do we shoot a quail, a capercailzie, or a landrail? If some people occasionally bag the two former species, certainly most have never even seen a landrail to-day. Yet publishers seem convinced that this wretched bird is popular game. For their enlightenment the irrepressible Hawker describes the best approach to landrail. 'Go behind a hedge near the swaths of corn, with two bones, one of which must be notched like a saw, the other plain; and by drawing the one down the serrated part of the other, you will produce a noise, which so far imitates their call, as often to draw them close to your place of concealment.' If game book sellers really believe that their clients pursue landrail, then they should make available a respectable stock of bones, plain and serrated.

But if not, it would be more to the point to devise, like the King, a register adapted to modern needs, for the royal game book presents a layout for general purposes which is the ideal answer. All the usual species of game are included for both highland and lowland sport, and sufficient columns for wildfowl are available to provide for all but exceptional occasions.

Here is a practical and sensible pattern for all game books. There is no column for fish in this book, but it is not a fishing book. There is no space for stags, for it is not a stalking book. There is nothing, however, to prevent anyone entering, in a wide blank column, trout, salmon, roedeer, wild turkeys, flamingos, or anything desired. And it will still look tidy and pleasing to the eye.

The King took a special interest in his woodcock records, and he noted down not only the day's bag of woodcock but his own personal score. Throughout his life, from the first woodcock he secured, he marked up his own total separately in red ink, immediately above the party's total, which was in ordinary ink.

He shot his first woodcock at Sandringham on December 27th, 1911. On that day he killed not only his first, but his second and third. There were six guns and the bag was 169 pheasants, 25

September 20th, 1927   GLAMIS   *Kingsmire* and *Linross Bog*

8   partridges Pat Glamis and myself
1   hare
1   rabbit
1   woodcock Fine. Snipe wild and patchy.
9 (7) snipe   Saw some old partridges.

20

---

hares, 167 rabbits, 56 duck, 1 teal, 1 various and 8 woodcock—
a grand winter's day. The young sportsman therefore got more
than his share, and three woodcock in a day, if you have never
got one before, is something of an event.

One can well imagine the delight of the young prince, the
warm approval of his older companions, the excitement with
which he must have gone to bed that evening. Many of us may
remember our first woodcock, but in most cases it was probably
the only one of the day. Not often has anyone on a first occasion
got more than any other member of an experienced party.

Perhaps it was this pleasurable reflection which prompted the
King's special records for woodcock. It would have been natural
to note under remarks 'my first woodcock'. But the temptation
to record that three out of the total bag of eight fell to the gun of
the young boy of the party was evidently irresistible, and the seed
of a special interest may well have been sown on that evening.
Henceforth he would always indicate the number of woodcock he
himself shot.

In the record of this single event resides a wealth of significance, for there is presented a picture that in many aspects is
strongly characteristic of the shooting King in later life. First there
was his zealousness and ardour, demonstrated by his prompt
satisfaction with his own score. This keenness never left him, and
to the end of his life it was enough simply to observe the counte-
nance of the King in the field to appreciate how deep and

December 27th, 1911   SANDRINGHAM   *Frankfort* and *Woodcock Wood*
169   pheasants   David, Harry Stonor, Edgey Knollys, Sir George
25   hares   Holford, Sir Arthur Davidson and myself
167   rabbits
8 (3) woodcock
56   wild duck
1   teal   My first woodcock.
1   various

427

strong was his capacity for enjoyment. The infectious nature of
this ardour is happily described by one of his lifelong companions
in a later chapter.

Again in the young boy, that evening in 1911, there emerged
his passion for accuracy and careful records. It was not enough to
record simply '8 woodcock'—it had to be five by the party and
three by himself. And yet another feature, his insistence on neatness was marked even then, and ensured for the great game book
perpetual tidiness. A pot of red ink had to be obtained for the
personal woodcock scores, and later this distinction was reserved
also for snipe.

In a character of such exacting standards it was inevitable later
on, when the opportunities of real sport came his way, that His
Majesty should have applied himself to the game with professional care and study. In boyhood days the necessary qualities of
the countryman artist were already present, and all that was required was that the chance and the example should present themselves.

This first woodcock event, in 1911, took place four years after
His Majesty started shooting with the muzzle-loader. He killed
one more woodcock during that season, and in January the following year added nine more, all shot at Sandringham. Thereafter a
steady average of woodcock fell to his gun, until the day of the
last entry on January 25th, 1952, when he shot three. The last
bird of all was Number 1055.

December 20th, 1919 SANDRINGHAM *Woodcock*
84   pheasants Papa, David, Harry, Sir Charles Cust and myself
14   rabbits
41 (13) woodcock
53   wild duck
2   teal
1   pigeon
3   various

198

                    (Making His Majesty's score of woodcock 100.)

A thousand woodcock is a sporting record of great quality when, as in this case, none were shot on 'woodcock shoots'. They were not secured in heavy bags in Ireland or the West of Scotland, but were ordinary migratory woodcock on ordinary shoots. Indeed, of this total of 1,055, no less than 928 were shot in Norfolk. And in all his days the King only secured double figures himself on three occasions. In 1919 he got 13 out of 41 with five guns, and in 1925 10 out of 35 with seven guns, on both occasions at Sandringham. At Lochinch in 1934 he shot 10 out of 16 with six guns.

These three days yielded only 33 birds. The remaining 1,022 were therefore bagged in single figures during woodland shoots, predominantly in Norfolk.

For a man of such profound enthusiasm as the King, one can judge with what warm contentment he must have entered a four-figure woodcock total for the first time. As recently as New Year's Day, 1951, during his last full season's shooting, he went out at Sandringham on a crisp and sunny winter's morning when his woodcock score to date was 998. Only two more wanted!

There were six guns and it was one of those happy Norfolk occasions, a family party after Christmas. During a day full of suspense His Majesty shot six of the 14 woodcock obtained, and that evening he sat down in his study to enter up the day's bag. Many times had he opened the scarlet-bound game book on such an evening, but this time it must have been with considerable

---

December 9th, 1925 CASTLE RISING *White Hills* and *Fowlers*

871	pheasants	Papa, Uncle Charles, David, Harry, Olav, Harry
37	partridges	Stonor and myself
41	hares	
36	rabbits	Lovely day. Birds flew well.
35 (10)	woodcock	Lots of woodcock.
3	pigeons	
6	various	

1,029 (Making the total over 200 woodcock.)

relish. As the hand filled in the figures 1,004, a tingle of pleasure would have been inescapable.

In the life of a sovereign of many peoples, and particularly of a great sovereign, it is naturally the events of national and universal importance for which posterity remembers him. A sporting biographer must not permit himself to overdramatise the minor incidents of sport, nor to accord to them prominence in the annals of royal history. Nevertheless, the subjects of King George the Sixth regarded him with such profound affection that it was often the personal and intimate events which provoked their warmest interest. Because he was so close to us our special attention was often reserved for his pleasures and his time off, and since his great love was shooting, it is not, perhaps, taking a disproportionate view to recognise a thousandth woodcock as a significant achievement in the life of a King.

The thousandth bird was bagged only in the year before his death. But for His Majesty's courage and strength of spirit in failing health, the red figures might well have remained in the threes. In such a fine game book this, to sporting men, would have been sad. But what must inevitably have become a keenly desired personal target for many years was achieved and passed handsomely. Those of us who share the King's tastes can share as well, and thankfully for his sake, the pleasure with which he must have made this notable entry.

In one other respect the King's woodcock achievement was distinguished. He belonged to that minority among sportsmen who have been fortunate enough to be presented with a chance of a right and left, and who have been sufficiently skilled to take advantage of it. During a covert drive after the war at Sandringham two woodcock came over him high above the trees, one on either side. He killed them both cleanly.

Confronted with such a record, the reader will readily surmise that the King was an exceptional performer at woodcock.

He was at all times a quick shot. He was one of those alert and nimble performers who had often killed his first bird, when partridge driving, before his neighbour had his gun into his shoulder.

Such a person is likely to kill more woodcock than the majority, for the secret of success with this perplexing creature is to act without hesitation. If you fire confidently at the first moment that seems appropriate, you will usually get your bird. If you lack boldness and wait for the bird to present itself more conveniently, or if you dwell on it during your swing, you will lose him time and again.

A woodcock is not a difficult bird to shoot by reason of its actual flight. It is, as a rule, slower than game birds and its flight almost as even. But it has got the habit, more than other birds, of doing the unexpected. It changes direction suddenly, without reason. It dips without warning in the open. Flying along an open ride, it steers suddenly for no apparent reason into the thickest branches. Its course is always absolutely unpredictable.

Therefore if you wait for these events to happen, or attempt to follow it with your gun, you will very likely pull the trigger a split second after it has turned sharply to a flank, and as you fire you are already aware that your pattern is going to be hopelessly off target. A lightning swing, however, amounting almost to a snap shot, is usually successful, for speed and confidence constitute the formula for good woodcock shooting.

This suited the King's style. He saw a woodcock and he shot it. Before he paused to consider where it was going, the bird was dead in the air. The King's accomplishment, through matchless co-ordination of eye and limb, of alertness and spontaneous reaction, was of the highest order.

This all who saw him shoot know well. But the simple

August 19th, 1935 GLAMIS *Rochel Hill* and *White Top*
    2   hares   Michael Lyon, Col. Malcolm Lyon and myself
129   rabbits
    6 (4) woodcock A very nice day though hot walking.
  20   grouse

---

157   (Making the score 500 woodcock.)

BALMORAL

LUNCHEON INTERLUDE
*The King with Sir Arthur Penn during a day's
grouse shooting at Balmoral*

statistician might claim that further evidence is available of his superiority.

The total of woodcock shot, as entered in his game book, was 4,312. The average number of guns for each day, throughout the length of the book, is six. The average number of woodcock per gun is, therefore, 718. But the King shot 1,055.

The conclusion which the statistician will readily draw is that His Majesty was an incomparably better marksman than those with whom he shot. Good as the King was, however, his friends and companions were also in the first flight, and it would not have been possible for any man to have established so significant a lead over expert competitors in the normal conditions of the shooting field. What is proved, therefore, by the fact that His Majesty shot far more than his share of woodcock, is that he had more opportunities than the rest of the party. And these opportunities are not found in the centre of a pheasant stand, nor in the best positions at a covert drive.

Here is testimony therefore that His Majesty was among the most gracious hosts in his realm, and, after arranging for the placing of his guests for a drive, he usually walked up with the line of beaters. He did not, as one might reasonably have supposed, occupy a specially marked point where the birds would be highest and most numerous, but was an example in every respect for all shooting hosts. And it is, of course, in the region of the beaters, close to cover, among the rides and the clumps, that the majority of woodcock are inclined to present themselves. Add to

---

January 1st, 1951   SANDRINGHAM   *Wolferton Wood* and *Dersingham Wood*

181	pheasants	Harry, E. Bacon, Fermoy, N. Gwatkin, Althorp and
10	hares	myself
18	rabbits	
14 (6)	woodcock	Fine but dull. Cold thaw. My thousandth woodcock.
10	pigeons	
2	various	

235

this the King's exceptional experience and his knowledge of his own ground, and it is hardly surprising that he was so frequently in the right place at the right time.

This gracious conduct is traditional in the royal family, and though King Edward the Seventh could not have claimed, nor even probably desired, to be a 'shooting sportsman' according to the Hawker pattern, most certainly he was as notable an example of consideration and kindness towards his guests as his grandson. Indeed the fundamental purpose of shooting to King Edward was largely as a medium of entertainment. He did not, lacking the shooting 'bug', desire anything particularly for himself, but he desired everything possible for his friends. Out shooting, 'King Edward was an ideal host. His was not the manner of polished civility which is so often merely a cloak for indifference. His extreme courtesy was the outcome not only of good breeding and good taste, but of genuine kindness of heart.'[1]

In the same manner the late King's kindness as a host was always being manifested. Any guest who was shy or nervous would be constantly encouraged and put at his ease, and His Majesty could never endure to cause embarrassment or discomfort to anyone. Once a young guest drove off from the door at Sandringham with such vulgar and thoughtless haste that he churned up the gravel on the drive as he went and stones were scattered on the grass. The King, watching from a window, was naturally incensed, and a member of the household, likewise annoyed, assured His Majesty that he would have a word with the offender. But a few moments later the King was imploring his *aide* to say nothing and to forget the matter, lest the young man should be made to feel uncomfortable.

His late Majesty had always a special welcome for children in the shooting field, for he liked to have them with him and never suggested that they should be kept at a distance. On one occasion he feared that two children who happened to be watching during a drive might get cold, and so he put them in his Land-rover and they just rode about with him for the rest of the afternoon. The

[1] Watson, *King Edward VII as a Sportsman.*

young princesses invariably came out with Her Majesty to join the
party at luncheon, and the presence of young children and the
family character of the shooting parties were among the attractive
features of Sandringham life.

In the same way he disliked intensely any unkindness to
animals, and he never could bear to see a dog beaten. He had a
strange attraction for dogs and they all went up to him as may
happen in a curious way with certain huntsmen. The King never
saw his own dogs, except on holiday, because he felt that he had
not sufficient time to exercise them in London.

Graciousness and good manners were as prominent a feature of
His Majesty's shooting life as his success with a gun, and he was
indeed an example which few others equal. A host who had entertained His Majesty on a Saturday would almost certainly re-
ceive a personal letter of thanks by express post on Monday
morning, and during his days as a guest he would never have
expected to be assigned favoured positions.

Of this kindness, modesty, and good nature perhaps the most
striking evidence is to be found in the game book itself. It is a remarkable fact, but from the first of its pages to the last, over a
period of forty-five years, there is not one comment by the King
regarding either his own prowess, nor a single mention of poor
form or failure by others. At the same time he must have been
frequently aware of both, and in so much shooting over his own
ground there must have been many occasions when he could have
wished a participant had done better. But this aspect was never
apparently of importance to him. The first object was that all the

---

January 25th, 1952 SANDRINGHAM *Appleton, Woodcock, Shernbourne*

52	pheasants	Philip, Euston, A. Penn (a.m.), W. Fellowes (p.m.),
4	hares	A. H. Bellingham (p.m.), R. Ralli (p.m.), Plunkett and
4	rabbits	myself
6 (3)	woodcock	
7	various	Dull, cold and still.

73   (The King's last woodcock, No. 1055.)

company should enjoy their day, and to have made a guest feel uncomfortable by seeming to observe his poor form would have been entirely out of character. In the same way, even in the private pages of the game book, it would have been contrary to His Majesty's gentler instincts to refer to such incidents.

The King was himself the greatest of all proof that we have indeed progressed to a nobler understanding, and completed almost 'the full circle'. On many estates before the first war it was the practice to count and record the number of birds killed by each gun at a stand, with what object, when so much is due to chance, the wind, or the light, it is beyond us to-day to comprehend. Nevertheless this custom provoked most undignified sentiments, and Lord Ripon described for us the antics of one of his guests. 'Two gentlemen were invited by me to shoot grouse at Studley. I was most anxious to see them compete in each other's company, for they were both very fine shots. Mr. B. fancied himself quite as good, if not better than, Mr. A., whilst I considered the latter the better of the two. I did not want to shoot myself, but during the first drive lay down in the heather behind A.'s box. There was a sharp sidewind blowing along the line of butts, and A., who was up-wind of B., dropped a considerable number of birds on to B.'s ground and the outskirts of it. The moment the drive was over A. went to pick up his birds up-wind, and I, who had remained hidden in the heather, saw B. come straight into A.'s ground, collect as many birds as he could carry, and return to his own ground, where he proceeded to drop them, leaving them to be picked up later. This happened several times during the day, but at the end of the afternoon, notwithstanding the depredations of B., A. beat him by something like eighty birds. Of course I never told either of them what I had seen.'[1]

Good fellowship in the shooting field seems to have been even more exceptional on another property, where Lord Ripon 'was much astonished to see a shooter bombarding the butt next to him with dead birds. As I approached I heard him shouting as he cast the birds at his neighbour, "Take the d—d lot! I don't care! Take

[1] Watson, *King Edward VII as a Sportsman.*

the lot, d—n you!" He was under the impression that his neighbour had picked up some of his birds—and he very likely had!'
This distasteful aspect of sport in bygone days would have earned
no sympathy from King George the Sixth.

From a study of this royal game book its author is revealed as
a warm-hearted companion, as a kindly neighbour and host, as a
learned countryman who was an integral part of his own lands,
and as a sportsman who was an artist—an artist to whom concentration, study and consistent skill were fundamentals for the
attainment of satisfaction. From the performance of His Majesty
all can learn many lessons. But first we must trace how these
particular lessons were learned by His Majesty.

III

ROUGH SHOOTING

With the woodcock we have trespassed forward into the times of the great expert, and we must now revert to early days once more and find His Majesty still doing as he was bid according to unruffled custom, standing in the line at Sandringham covert shoots. He accepted all this as a matter of routine, but it made surprisingly little impression on him, and in all the years until 1921 the King never entered a single observation of interest against his game-book entries. The love of accuracy was demonstrated from the start and the details of the bag and the names of the party were always faithfully recorded, but there is no comment on what transpired during the day, nor on any unexpected interludes that arose.

In 1921, however, there was a sudden change, and this seems to have been the year of awakening. All at once we find remarks creeping into the game book—observations about the wind, mention of gales, of birds doing this and that, of certain drives succeeding and elsewhere of failures. Very soon no event was entered up without a supporting observation. It is astonishing how the

---

September 29th, 1921   GLAMIS   *Haughs of Cossins*

9	partridges	Michael Lyon, David Lyon and myself
1	hare	
4	rabbits	A rough walk.
1 (1)	snipe	
2	wild duck	
4	pigeons	

21

scales seem to have fallen suddenly from the King's eyes and he saw before him a richer landscape of unknown possibilities. The sport to which he had been brought up seems to have been as lustreless to him as an ancient and uncleaned oil-painting. He was accustomed to its presence, like a dark picture on the wall, but never paused to study it because the detail and the colour were obscured. Suddenly, as if the professional restorer had done his work, the sombre film was wiped from the canvas and vivid colours glowed where none were thought to exist. Detail appeared out of the blackness, and the whole composition assumed a new meaning and more exciting purpose.

And the restorer in this instance was Glamis.

The King paid his first shooting visit to Glamis in September 1921. There were three days' partridge shooting which averaged 120 brace, but the most significant day was the fourth, when the King with his two brothers-in-law had a rough walk and bagged 9 partridges, 1 hare, 4 rabbits, 1 snipe, 2 duck, and 4 pigeons. In itself this is nothing remarkable, but it was, in fact, the first rough maraud the King ever enjoyed. This day marked the start of an entirely new chapter in his shooting life, which henceforth was punctuated regularly by a wealth of rough and varied days. Glamis offered the King new opportunities which had never before come his way, and urged on by the tireless enthusiasm of the Bowes-Lyon family the whole aspect of his recreation was altered from then on. The somewhat tedious repetition of formal and very similar entries in his game book during the first fourteen years gives way after 1921 to a varied pattern of diverse experiences.

The influence of the Glamis connection cannot be over-emphasised, since as the seasons passed it was in the Glamis pattern of sport that the King found a new and lasting appeal—mixed and varied days, snipe drives, and so on. This was the phase when

---

August 31st, 1923 GLAMIS *Back Strip of Policies*
41 rabbits   Lord Strathmore, David Lyon and myself
                 We shot for two hours.

the King, so to speak, went back to school. He discovered suddenly that he 'knew only one-third of his art', and he resolved at
once to acquire knowledge of the other two-thirds. To the rough
training which followed he took like a duck to water, and soon
acquired that finer insight and understanding which a season of
formal shooting cannot satisfy.

Thus his outlook became more critical, and his standards more
exacting, and that the measure of his appreciation was not a
numerical one is demonstrated by his game-book notes. At Sandringham in 1921 after three good days' covert shooting, the King
remarked, 'Birds flew very badly.' After another day which produced 420 pheasants we come to the interesting comment that
'nothing went right'. Yet next season, during a visit to Glamis,
76 grouse only were killed by four guns, and His Majesty observed, 'A good day and birds came well.' During the same week
he was out for half a day with his brother-in-law, David Bowes-
Lyon, and noted 'An excellent morning's walk. Snipe very wild'
—the bag was 5 snipe and 2 duck.

It has to be admitted that before 1921 game-book entries which
did not feature at least a three-figure total, and occasionally four,
could almost be counted on the fingers of the hand, but after 1921
a succession of two-figure entries, and often singles, became a
customary feature. The parties, after grouse, hares, rabbits, duck,
snipe and teal, consisted usually of His Majesty, Lord Strathmore,
and Michael or David Bowes-Lyon.

In August 1923 four days at Glamis yielded 62, 30, 58 and 56
head. Towards the end of the month, after some good days grouse
driving elsewhere in Scotland, the King returned once more to

---

September 28th, 1922 GLAMIS *Newton*
96 partridges David Lyon, Arthur Penn and myself
12 hares
 2 rabbits
 1 pigeon   We had some good drives.

III

Glamis and this time four days yielded 57, 23, 41 and 8 head. On the last day he tramped almost as many miles. On another occasion His Majesty noted that it was 'very wet and windy with few birds', whilst on the following he had 'a better day, Syke's drive a new way went well'. It is engaging to note how the King grappled from the outset with his new experiences on the hill and in the bogs of Glamis with unquenchable enthusiasm, and he was never concerned about the quantity of birds encountered, but only with the cause and effect of the manoeuvres. 'Why? Simply because, whether you kill many or few birds, the smaller total will probably require as great an outlay of patience, skill, and endurance to obtain it, as the larger.' [1]

On a September day in Yorkshire in 1923 there were 'very few birds. Black Ark was a total failure'. On another day 'the last drive was spoilt by a buzzard over the moor', and the next entry revealed 'another day spoilt by mist, only 3 drives', and yet again they 'only shot in forenoon. Another day spoilt by rain'. One can certainly sympathise with the King's feelings when he wrote, following a day after grouse, 'the birds went everywhere but over us'. But there is only one hint of frustration, when with perhaps tensely gripped quill he wrote, 'Very thick covert, too many dogs, very few rabbits and very heavy rain.' Certainly it does not sound an agreeable form of entertainment.

The big occasions did not, of course, come to an end. Some good bags were made on Strathmore property, particularly at Holwick in Yorkshire, and at Sandringham in the 'twenties a thousand head was still frequent. But His Majesty was always ready to expend more energy, to get his boots waterlogged, to get his clothing sodden in the mist, or to strip to his shirt sleeves beneath the piping sun of early autumn up the glens and round the lochs at Glamis. It had become all one to him. Every day was approached in a different spirit, tuned to the occasion. The most interesting development was that the big days, which seem to have failed so ignominiously to inspire him for some fifteen years, could now even provoke comments in the game book and were frequently

[1] Sir R. Payne-Gallwey, *Letters to Young Shooters.*

honoured with such attentions. The birds were now recorded as
being either high or low, the weather was observed to have some
influence on the routine, and the most typical of West Norfolk
bombardments were no longer simply grey half-tones, but dif-
fered widely in hue and light and shade. Even Dersingham Wood,
that intriguing forest of 'snowberrry, privets, and the like', was
on one occasion found worthy of a mention in despatches, for on
a day there in 1924 it was 'fine, but cold and windy', and, almost
unbelievably, 'the birds flew well for a change'. The wind, we
venture to think, must surely have been of gale-force.

In these years there emerged a new sportsman in His Majesty.
He joined the ranks of great sportsman-naturalists, who, by their
hard-won experience in an individual capacity—solitary man
against bird or beast and the ground and the elements—transcend
the majority of their contemporaries. There are, of course, a handful of such men in every generation, but certain names will always
spring to the mind and will shine forever in sporting history,
largely by virtue of their literary gifts and the classical works of
instruction which they have bestowed upon the shooting world
—such names as Peter Hawker, Abel Chapman, Sir Ralph
Payne-Gallwey—men who in every respect combined all the
qualities already emphasised in these pages. They were princes of
the art of shooting, to be joined now by a king. These men were
artists indeed—they were close to their country and to the wild
creatures that inhabited it, and because of their sensitive and
cultured appreciation of natural things they developed an un-
surpassed gift for descriptive prose. Abel Chapman described
beautifully in a sentence what is missed by non-wildfowlers who

---

September 27th, 1923   HOLWICK   *Black Ark, Silver Band*
  3 rabbits   Lord Strathmore, Jock, Michael and David Lyon, Wisp
  1 snipe   Leveson-Gower and myself
  2 black game
343 grouse   A very nice day.

349

---

remain abed in the morning '. . . that impressive change—the lifting of the night's mantle from the earth. Gradually grew these first rays, and soon the whole east was aglow, gleaming across parched plains, as the glorious morn awakened.'[1] This fine passage must stir the mind of every duck shooter.

Peter Hawker was not only one of the greatest wildfowlers and naturalists ever to pull on his waders and push a punt along the foaming tideway, he was an accomplished musician as well, a connoisseur, and a writer. In writing of his classical work of instruction, Payne-Gallwey, one of his few equals, said, 'Foremost and unrivalled stands the work of that father of wildfowl-shooting, Colonel Peter Hawker.' That is a heartening tribute paid by one great expert to another, and therein is demonstrated one of the agreeable attributes of true shooting sportsmen and wildfowlers. They are men of humility and give credit gladly where it is due, though this is not always the case in other fields of 'sport', and it was certainly far from being so in the case of Lord Ripon's friends on the moors. But in no man was it more notably characteristic than in His Majesty, who, whilst acquiring unrivalled experience and knowledge himself, yet remained unassuming and humble in sporting company, eager to listen and anxious to derive from the experience of his companions whatever knowledge might be acquired.

Nothing, except how to shoot straight at one type of target, can be learned by the man standing in a line of guns, and one can feel nothing but compassion for the offspring of 'great houses' who

[1] Abel Chapman, *Wild Spain*.

November 25th, 1922   St. Paul's Walden Bury

620	pheasants	Lord Strathmore, Lord Hampden, Jock Lyon, Michael
16	partridges	Lyon, David Lyon and myself
15	hares	
8	rabbits	
7	various	The birds came well as usual.

666

are given no other opportunity. As Hawker said, they learn only
a third of it all, and elsewhere, warming to his point, he declares
that they know only one-twentieth. 'After I had shot for more
than thirty years, not a season, no, not even a month or a week
elapsed, without my discovering that I had been previously
ignorant of some trifle or other. If, therefore, a person feels himself above hearing an opinion in this, as well as in every other art,
he decidedly gives the greatest and most positive proof of his own
deficiency and narrowness of conception. Safely, however, may it
be said, that in field sports, as well as in other pursuits, there are
thousands who fancy that no one can show them anything, when
they have literally not learnt above a twentieth part of their art.'
The King quickly discovered that he was ignorant of many trifles
and therefore sought to correct this. And he was never 'above
hearing an opinion', but with eager and boyish enthusiasm welcomed such expressions from all with whom he came into contact.

Alone, or with one or two companions, one may learn for a
lifetime. No member of the royal house had ever before had profound experience with a shotgun, but His Majesty in the 'twenties
learned as much as any in his kingdom. He was often alone and
out for a whole day collecting perhaps less than twenty head, but
as a diversion this held as much fascination for him as being continuously confined to a butt. 'I was alone' became a common an-
notation in the game book after 1921, and it is evident from the
records that when a day's shooting was not arranged, and the

October 4th, 1923	GLAMIS	*Collie Drum*
6	pheasants	Lord Strathmore, Pat Glamis, Arthur Penn, Michael
233	partridges	and David Lyon and myself
20	hares	
2	rabbits	
1 (1)	woodcock	A nice lot of birds. Very cold N.E. wind sprang up.
1	snipe	
2	teal	
2	pigeons	

267

other members of the family were not available, then the King departed for the day on his own into the remote recesses of the highlands. One October day at Glamis he went forth and bagged after a full day 11 rabbits, 3 pigeons and 1 various, and commented, 'a very nice walk I had alone'. Hardly a king's bag, it must be owned, but there is no telling from the score what was the quality of the enjoyment. But five days after this he was at Sandringham, when the day's sport yielded 77 pheasants, 1,117 partridges, 57 hares, 4 rabbits, 3 pigeons and 1 various—a magnificent bag, for partridges are truly wild and sporting creatures and there can be no scepticism about the magnitude of this event. Yet the King displayed only equal enthusiasm over either engagement, and after this exhilarating experience was content to note, 'Perfect day for driving. Never seen so many birds. Heavy thunderstorm in last drive.'

The longer the odds the more sweet is success, and enjoyment of sport is related directly to the quality of skill, energy, luck and companionship which is incidental to the occasion. 'We went to different places mainly for snipe. Great fun.' 'Spent the day there and did the loch twice. The snipe in the sewage farm drove well.' 'V. nice day. Early morning flight and a good walk.' As one scans the royal pages such observations are abundant. They are remarks which could have been made by the most humble enthusiast, and which echo our own experiences. Of a reigning monarch they are perhaps least typical.

In most things in life one learns by mistakes, and in these early days there are notes of many failures. After a rough day at snipe and teal, for example, the King wrote: 'Wind was wrong, and nothing we tried succeeded.' On a day in 1930 at Glamis 'the bogs

---

August 12th, 1925	GLAMIS	*Powmire Bogs*
2 (2) snipe		I was alone
4	wild duck	
2	teal	Fairweather and Young were with me.
—		Standing Stone and Loch-na-Dance Bogs.
8		Duck and teal were very wild. Fine.
—		

were empty and the duck avoided us.' In the same season, but on another visit, there were 'not many snipe in and very wild. Nothing went right all day.' And on another day, when he was alone in the wilds at Glamis, he killed, in all, 19 head and commented, 'Owing to N.E. wind, duck very wild and never came near me. A good many snipe in. Lost 3.'

Rough shooting may also be enjoyed on a more impressive scale in rough and varied country, and the King both on his own ground and elsewhere enjoyed many exceptional occasions in later years. Perhaps none surpassed, however, three truly remarkable days in 1934 at Lochinch in Western Scotland.[1] Lochinch is wonderful shooting country, comprising lochs, woodland, moors, marshes and arable fields. By the use of a car there is practically nothing in the game book which may not be secured in a single day, and the indefatigable enthusiasm of its owner has earned for this glorious ground a renowned reputation for rough shooting with a capital S and an even more distinctive R. It has been said that on a shooting visit, of whatever duration, the guest is expected to start and finish shooting in the dark. At all events this was the King's own experience.

As Duke of York he was scheduled, being Colonel of the Scots Guards, to attend an Old Comrades' dinner in Stranraer on November 13th. The opportunity was taken therefore to combine a little sport at Lochinch with the reunion of the Old Comrades, and the King with a friend in attendance left Euston on the night of the 12th. His companion had had considerable experience of Lochinch, and on his advice therefore His Royal

[1] The home of the Earl of Stair.

August 27th, 1924 GLAMIS *Rochil Hill*

1	hare	Morven Bentinck, David Lyon and myself
157	rabbits	
1	snipe	
4	grouse	A lovely fine day. Plenty of rabbits.

163

Highness was waiting in his carriage at 5.30 a.m. on the 13th as the train drew into Stranraer with his waders already pulled on and his gun practically loaded. These precautions received early vindication, for their host was waiting at the station with cocoa and buns and a high impatience to be on the move. There was a first faint light in the eastern sky as they floated away in a pre-1914 vintage Rolls to a beat called Knock. There the party collected 2 greylag geese and 10 golden plover before the guests ever set eyes on the house in which they were to stay.

For the rest of three days every hour of each day, and some of each night, was employed to the full in diverse activities over every sort of ground and water. At one stage His Royal Highness left the ground altogether and was placed in a tree-top platform for pigeons. The result of all this was the three bags of most exceptional quality shown here.

November 13th		November 14th		November 15th	
15	pheasants	7	pheasants	32	partridges
2	partridges	17	partridges	11	hares
9	hares	21	hares	4	rabbits
29	rabbits	70	rabbits	16 (10)	snipe
4 (1)	woodcock	24 (4)	snipe	1	wild duck
6 (2)	snipe	44	wild duck	5	teal
19	wild duck	25	teal	6	wigeon
20	teal	6	wigeon	3	pigeon
32	wigeon	9	pigeon	26	golden plover
1	pigeon	1	golden plover	2	greylag geese
12	black game	4	various	1	various
19	grouse	—		—	
12	golden plover	228		107	
2	greylag geese	—		—	
4	various				

186

LOCHINCH	first day	Knock, Round Wood and New Luce
	second day	Loch Battloch, Culhorn and Balyett
	third day	Knock and West Corsewall
	Party	Stair, Dalrymple, Cis. Dalrymple-Hamilton, W. Balfour, Tommy Coke and myself

These bags might well have been even more prolific if the weather, for this type of sport, had been more suitable. Tommy Coke,[1] who accompanied His Royal Highness from London, afterwards made the following note in his game book: 'Three of the best and most enjoyable days' shooting imaginable, but unfortunately the weather was much too fine, sun and frost every day with not a cloud in the sky, no wind and a moon; in fact the worst possible flighting weather. Altogether very unusual for the west coast of Scotland. Nevertheless we got 71 duck the first evening on Knock flight ponds and we saw a good many greylag flying about in the distance. H.R.H. was shooting very well indeed. We motored well over 60 miles every day.'

Days such as these are the routine at Lochinch. That they were very much to the King's taste was proved by his frequent reference to them in after years.

And so, as the seasons passed, the great shooting expert was made, largely in the early years at Glamis. And that he was made from a royal prince with prodigious experience of vast bags, who was already a first-class shot, is a unique phenomenon.

[1] Now 5th Earl of Leicester.

August 15th, 1925	GLAMIS *Forfar Loch*
15 (14) snipe	Fairweather and myself
15 wild duck	
5 teal	A nice 3½ hours in the forenoon. Several snipe and duck
2 various	in. I walked, F. went in the boat. Fine and warm.
37	

IV

FLIGHTING

The more I see of wildfowl-shooting the more am I convinced how slightly is success therein achieved by luck, and how very much this sport is dependent upon experience and a skilful use of the favourable moment, whatever be the time, trouble and money expended thereon by its votaries.

SIR R. PAYNE-GALLWEY, 1896

The degree of a man's taste and accomplishment in the shooting field can often be measured by the degree of his interest in wild duck, and also by the manner in which he goes after them. The romantic among shooters likes to be called a wildfowler, and a wildfowler shoots duck only in a certain way. The difference between the true artist among shooters and the casual *chasseur* is that one is a wildfowler and one is not.

What is it about wildfowl that fires the spirit of imaginative sportsmen so much more effectively than game birds? It is the fact that the various species which the genus includes are not local residents, and that you can never know for certain whether they are with you or not. There is a strong element of chance—here to-day and gone to-morrow; and gone, either to the next parish only, or just as likely to parched plains in Spain or Africa, or, on the return movement, to the grim whiteness of the Arctic. Thus there is a further element of mystery, for their movements are often unexpected, and when you are least anticipating it, there, to thrill you, are duck in quantity where yesterday there were none.

This wildfowler's element of doubt and mystery is shared by ornithologists alike, and for them, too, the international travellers, or 'migrants' of ornithological parlance, are more intriguing than residents. However diverting a bullfinch or a barn owl, a kestrel or a robin, they are little more of a novelty to the birdwatcher than his domestic pets, for they are always about; if they are to be studied it can be done at leisure and convenience, and there is no urgency about it. But in spring and autumn the mixed and varied members of the observer corps, binoculars and pocket-books at the ready, are out in force to patrol the sea-walls and the estuaries; and the arrival of a traveller from afar, stirring in the mind's eye images of sun-baked *marisma* or creaking ice-floe, is an event of incalculable fascination, be it an American pectoral sandpiper or simply a common reed-warbler. Even the call of the first cuckoo tends to freeze half the population in its tracks, to listen in awed wonder and then to pen a hasty letter to the local press.

Wild duck of all species therefore intrigue both ornithologists and sportsmen, for even in Hyde Park the observer can wonder from whence the tufted duck have arrived—to what nationality were they born, how many hundreds of miles have they traversed, and how long will they remain before moving on? In the same way for the owner of a stretch of water, however moderate and circumscribed, it is a cause for constant speculation and hope— yes, *hope* above all—that his own special reserve will be favoured by these intrepid travellers who course the world's airlines according to their instinct, the elements, and a host of other contingencies beyond the wit or control of man. 'Hope indeed!' as Payne-Gallwey aptly observed, 'if *hope* would bring us fowlers good sport, there would soon be no ducks left to shoot at.'

In the face of all this excitement and uncertainty, how then can

---

September 27th, 1922   GLAMIS   *Warren Pond, etc.*

7 (1)	snipe	Michael Lyon, David Lyon, Arthur Penn and myself
6	wild duck	
3	teal	
7	pigeons	
1	various	

—

24

—

a known quantity of pheasants, or a known number of partridge coveys, provoke the intense degree of eager anticipation felt when we splash forward into a lonely wilderness of mudflat, swamp or reed-bed? In the case of His Majesty this keen sensation of anticipation, of eagerly looking forward to the event, was one of the most delightful features of his leisure. No man was more sensitive to the romantic and stirring features of the chase.

And this aspect surely, that of doubt and wonder about the movement of migratory duck, has not only intrigued every naturalist and sportsman in history, but must have fired the imagination of that other English king who constructed a haven in the midst of his capital especially to lure the various species of wildfowl out of the skies, which in those days were clear and smogless like the bracing heavens of farthest Norfolk. Charles, in spirit and thought, was also a wildfowler at heart.

King George the Sixth became an enthusiastic wildfowler. The more common usage of this term to-day denotes one who haunts the saltings and muds along the sea coast, with a 'stanchion-gun' or some other eccentric weapon. But it is as appropriately applied to the inland flight-shooter, and it was in this category that the King attained a distinctive eminence.

To the cream of shooting men wildfowling is the finest perfection of sport. Of all targets, however majestic or diverting they may be in the case of game birds, it is the flighting duck which is incomparable. It is wildfowl which make the heart beat faster, which, in blizzard or storm, warm the cockles and evoke tense excitement. At the best of game shoots, driving rain or paralysing cold inevitably disheartens the best of us. But in the presence of an approaching duck at flight time these inclemencies seem in

---

October 10th, 1928   GLAMIS   *The Warren*

3 (2)	snipe	Pat Glamis, Michael and David Lyon and myself
20	wild duck	
4	teal	An early morning flight. Too fine and still. Duck did not
—		come in.

27
—

some manner to enhance the magic of the hour. Wildfowlers, if they be as well acknowledged exponents in all fields of the sport, and if, in spite of their opportunity, they choose a flight before all else, then they are the fortunate *élite* among its adherents whose sensitiveness and insight afford them the true richness of enjoyment with the gun. For even without the migratory element, there is still one fundamental difference between duck-shooting (as it should be conducted) and game-shooting.

In the case of game-shooting we are creating an artificial circumstance. Birds which, if left in peaceful occupation, would be doing something else are forcibly despatched in a predetermined direction towards the expectant armoury. There should be no surprise (though, Lord forgive us, there often is) because the battery has already been put 'in the picture'—where to stand, which way to face, from whence the birds will approach; and from sounds and portents the individual can usually judge the moment at which he must bestir himself and pay attention. The men who drive the birds, or big game or anything else, can do this expertly or inefficiently, but practically all that is asked of the man with the weapon is to point it in the right direction.

Not so with proper duck-shooting, or 'flighting'. Here the bird is performing its natural round, it is doing what it desires to do on its own. And the wildfowler, by his knowledge and cunning and his willingness to accept the conditions in which his quarry naturally operates, seeks to intercept it. He inserts himself at a point where, through experience or observation, he believes the bird will arrive, and he waits for it. There is no artificial feature in this pursuit. Thus the objective is not to perform a brilliant shot, but to be in the right place at the right time, inconspicuously, and to secure the quarry expertly in spite of the conditions which may comprise near-darkness. And the realisation that even the first part of this objective has been achieved, as a blurred dark form twists towards you in the half-light, stirs the deepest instinct of primeval man. This time we are outwitting the wild.

This method of shooting duck, by 'flighting', was well understood over a century ago and was described for sportsmen in

Hawker's classic. Duck 'show excellent sport to anyone who has patience to wait for them. Our sporting writers in general have given no further directions for duck-shooting, than to walk quietly up a brook, and shoot them as they rise.' But whatever sporting writers may have said, in any generation, many people still think that to 'blow up' duck is not only good fun, but the most rewarding method. The great authorities seem, indeed, to have been wasting their time and their ink for all the notice that has generally been taken of their advice. 'One of the usual methods of obtaining a few wild ducks, and frightening perhaps a great many, is for a party of shooters to steal silently up to a small pool and take position round it, under cover of trees and bushes, or behind reed screens erected for the purpose of affording a near approach unperceived by the wildfowl.

'The ducks are put on wing when everybody is ready. There is one grand fusillade at the birds as they rise, very few come down, and the survivors probably desert their haunt for a week or more.

'Supposing a pool of three or four acres holds a hundred wild duck; surround it as you like with half a dozen good marksmen; flush the birds and let the sportsmen blaze away as they will; I warrant they will not kill a score before the ducks bid a long *addio*. Yet I would engage to kill sixty of the hundred to my own gun the first *suitably* stormy day, if I were permitted to post myself in good concealment by the waterside to shoot them as they returned one by one, or in small parties, during the day.'[1] This passage refers to daytime flighting which, though offering more

[1] Sir R. Payne-Gallwey, *Letters to Young Shooters.*

August 17th, 1929 GLAMIS *Warren Pond*
  3 rabbits   Michael Lyon and myself
 21 wild duck
  1 pigeon   An evening flight. It poured in sheets the whole time. Not
 —   many duck about.
 25
 —

infrequent chances than dawn or dusk, is nevertheless of a similar science.

Writers and their books, perhaps fortunately for the bird's sake, have exercised little influence over the shooting community. Possibly this is accounted for by the unending glut of repetitive publications and by the irresistible temptation of so many authors to describe with dramatic unreality the more picturesque aspects of wildfowl-shooting. 'Duck-shooting is much talked of and written about, but it is in my experience a very uncertain sport, notwithstanding the artistic pictures I have seen relating thereto, and the glowing accounts I have read about it.'[1] If this sentiment was expressed in the last century, how much greater must be the true fowler's scepticism to-day, when motor-cars, aeroplanes, drainage schemes and other developments have reduced the duck population so severely. Yet, let's face it, it is just as tedious to read of a dull or unfruitful expedition, and even more aggravating to hear of inefficiency, lost opportunities and failure. What every student wishes to learn is how the knowledge and experience of the masters has met with success, and for this reason the classics survive, and the amateur biographies wither and die like the frozen reed-beds wherein their inspiration was born. Thus we are fortunate and privileged now to learn from a king among masters, and to read of the successes and stirring experiences which rewarded his patience and study.

Whenever a man, be he sovereign or one of his humble subjects, has been converted from a 'dabbler' in sport to a true sportsman, he has learned at once that he should wait for duck, and not

[1] *Ibid.*

August 2nd, 1930 GLAMIS *Warren Pond*

4	snipe	David Lyon, R. V. Brooke and myself
12	wild duck	
7	teal	
—		Evening flight. Very little came in although we waited
23		from 7.0 till 10.0 p.m.
—		

chase them. The King, as all know, was among the Olympians of
the shooting world. But when we remember Dersingham Wood
and royal shooting as it had been presented to him as a boy, it is a
fine thought for shooting enthusiasts that the King of England
was an experienced wildfowler.

However duck shooting was, like rough shooting, an interest
which His Majesty acquired unusually late in his shooting life, and
it was, in fact, fourteen years after he first handled a gun before he
ever waited for a flighting duck. The King was brought up to
shoot under his father, and until 1936, when his father died, the
royal estates were under parental management. King George the
Fifth, as we have already remarked, was a champion of the age at
game-shooting, but he had little knowledge of, nor inclination
for, flighting. Thus none was arranged.

Had King George the Fifth not been interested in shooting it is
likely that much of the responsibility and initiative for the direction of sport would have devolved upon his sons, and in this event
the Duke of York might have had many new enterprises to pro-
mote. But the fact remains that his father was extremely interested,
and exercised a close and constant supervision over shooting on
all the properties. Thus the Duke of York had in some degree,
during his father's lifetime, only the status of a guest on the royal
estates. There was a great deal of shooting offered on any free day
that the princes might have, but it was all highly organised and
the general pattern and method already determined.

Like rough shooting, his ultimate interest in duck evolved
from personal events unrelated to sport, and it was again the
Glamis connection which opened up an entirely new vista. Whilst
the bogs were tramped for snipe and teal, the lochs were also
flighted at both ends of the day, and a new stretch of water of
some twenty-five acres was constructed by the bare hands of the
family, which became a notable haunt of both duck and geese.[1]
Thus the royal brother-in-law enjoyed for the first time proper
flighting, and acquired greater knowledge and experience of wildfowl than in all the years of *grandes battues*. One of the best

[1] Warren Pond, referred to elsewhere.

features of the Glamis days was that, more often than not, 'we flighted in the evening'.

And there was yet one more such thread which was to lead the King into a landscape of reed-bed, marsh and wildfowl. The brother-in-law of Michael Bowes-Lyon, one of the King's new and constant companions with the gun, was Harry Cator, the owner of Ranworth Broad in Norfolk, and one of the finest fen-men, naturalists and wildfowlers of all time. This particular relationship was to cause regular entries in the duck columns of the King's game book for the rest of his life.

To turn back the pages once more and to introduce for the last time shooting as it was practised in previous reigns, we should ponder briefly on certain duck days which, to most of us now, would seem entirely foreign to our inclinations. During the first part of the present century, on many estates which featured a lake or stretch of water, large numbers of 'wild duck' were reared for each season's sport. To-day the rearing of duck for shooting is, to many wildfowlers, definitely not cricket. A duck for the true gunner is a denizen of wild spaces, a strong seasoned traveller which spans the continents and oceans, and which, by a combination of appropriate weather and the gunner's comprehension, and a marked degree of good fortune, it is hoped to bag as a climax to prolonged effort and study.

October 14th, 1929 SANDRINGHAM *The Marshes*

152	pheasants	Fritz Ponsonby, Wigram and myself
11	partridges	
29	hares	
13	rabbits	A lovely day. Plenty of duck and teal about in the creeks,
2 (2)	snipe	and many wild pheasants.
38	wild duck	
5	teal	
1	wigeon	
13	pigeon	
3	various	

267

To slay a duck, even if it may be the genuine article, *Anas platyrhynchos Linnaeus*, which has but recently been shepherded into the world by keeper Smith or underkeeper Brown, and bribed by liberal rations of maize or barley to remain in the locality where it first played nursery games chasing water-boatmen, is to the purist a mockery of the most refined art of the scatter-gun.

This was, however, the popular conception of duck-shooting in the reign of King Edward. It is enough to quote this passage: 'In 1908 the ducks were disappointing, in consequence of the unsatisfactory nature of the ice, which was not strong enough to bear the men who had to put the birds up, and was too strong for a boat to pass through; for, as readers are probably aware, the method of shooting is to make duck fly when they are inclined to settle, and as they circle round higher and higher, till often altogether out of shot, those that are in reach of the guns afford excellent sport.'[1]

If that is not enough to induce apoplexy in the modern fowler, herewith a final broadside. 'I was here shown (on Virginia Water) an ingenious mode of sweeping down the wildfowl, in large quantities, by Mr. Turner, Her Majesty's keeper, who, in his younger days, was a great performer in the fens. His plan for killing the wildfowl here was to fix a great many large guns parallel to the edge of the lake and to cover them over with grass. He planted them about a hundred yards apart; and had a long wire from the trigger of the foremost gun to the butt of the next one behind it; and so on. By this means he had only to plant, and then cock, all his guns; and, by pulling off the first with some

[1] Watson, *King Edward VII as a Sportsman*.

August 10th, 1927	GLAMIS *Forfar Loch*
16 (11) snipe	David Lyon and myself
7 wild duck	
—	A forenoon. Very few duck and snipe in. Reeds and
23	grass not yet cut, and very wet.
—	

hundred yards of line, he opened on the fowl an almost instanta-
neous running fire which swept the whole edge of the lake, where,
after their nightly feed, the birds generally came to take shelter, or
to sun themselves on a fine frosty day.'[1]

However, we must not be led through these reflections into a
presumptuous or impertinent condemnation of duck-rearing at
Sandringham in the reign of King George the Fifth. It was, after
all, a conventional feature of the times on many great shoots, and
we should no more say it was wrong, even though we may feel
we have in the meantime progressed to a more sensitive understanding, than we would say our grandparents were totally in-
sensitive to beauty because of our distaste for Victorian Gothic
architecture. *Chacun à son goût.*

The whole topic is only of interest here because it is so abundantly clear on which side of the fence the late King stood. Before
his father died, Sandringham provided duck by Smith or Brown.
After his accession, duck-rearing was abandoned and the new
flight ponds and splashes provided flighting wild duck by natural
agencies as far removed as the wastes of Scandinavia and perhaps
Siberia.

The King does not note the day on which he shot his first
duck.

[1] Peter Hawker, *Guns and Shooting.*

October 5th, 1927	GLAMIS *Sprottie, Linross* and *Forest Muir*
2 pheasants	Pat Glamis, David Lyon and myself
3 partridges	
2 hares	
9 rabbits	We went to different places, mainly for snipe. Fine.
19 (9) snipe	Great fun.
4 wild duck	
3 teal	
1 pigeon	
4 grouse	
1 golden plover	

48

On January 6th, 1908, the third occasion on which he ever ventured forth with a gun, one duck was killed in a small bag secured by himself and the Prince of Wales, but the King does not claim this bird. His first duck was probably shot three seasons later (there were no duck entries in the meantime) on December 27th, 1911, when six guns shooting over the Frankfort beat at Sandringham killed 427 head, including 56 mallard. This incidentally was the same day on which the King killed his first woodcock, one of the three, out of a total of eight, which has already been described. It is surprising that the King did not note 'my first duck', but it would be more surprising if he had not shot at least one of the fifty-six. The excitement of the woodcock achievement may well have monopolised all his thoughts—at all events, in view of the great records of which these two incidents were the beginning, the King's first woodcock and first duck accord to this single day a special distinction. Thereafter duck were shot regularly during covert shooting at Sandringham.

The discovery by His Majesty that the best way to shoot duck is to flight them was made at Glamis. On September 27th, 1922, a typical expedition round Warren Pond resulted in 7 snipe, 6 mallard, 3 teal, 7 pigeons and 1 various. The King makes no mention of flighting on this occasion in his game book, but David Bowes-Lyon, in his own book, remarked, 'flight a failure'. It is certain that this was the first occasion that the King actually waited for a duck to flight, as opposed to waiting for it to be hustled over his head by a beater.

Duck-flighting became thereafter a regular feature of the

December 9th, 1929 WOODBASTWICK *Ranworth Flood*

11	mallard	Harry Cator, Tim Birkin, Colin McLean, Harry Brown
1	gadwall	and myself
26	tufted duck	
23	pochard	Evening flight. Fine. Strong S.W. wind. Few mallard
5	various	came; mostly pochard.

66

Glamis visits, but it was not until 1929 that the King enjoyed his first duck flight proper on the Norfolk scale. On December 9th he went to stay with Harry Cator at Ranworth and at the evening flight on the Flood five guns picked 61 duck, including 11 mallard, 1 gadwall, 26 tufted duck and 23 pochard. In the morning they bagged on Ranworth and Cockshoot Broads 96 duck. The full bag was 84 mallard, 1 wigeon, 3 shoveler, 7 teal and 1 pintail.

By Ranworth standards these may not be red-letter occasions, but they were enough to introduce the King to an entirely new feature of the shooting scene. For the first time he saw a shoot, or a property, which was mainly a duck shoot. As a Norfolk neighbour, such places henceforth were regularly honoured by his participation in their fixtures.

The King now found himself a part of that splendid wild-fowler's setting so beloved by its devotees: the world of long waders and thick clothing; of punts, poles and oars; of torches and dogs hunting in the darkness; of ripples gently lapping the bows and the whispering of the wind in the rushes. This was a new world for His Majesty, and one so much more intriguing than that beside covert and hedgerow. Here was mystery in the early darkness and drama as the day is born, romance as the light fades once more—and at all times rewarding companionship derived from sharing experiences which call for endurance, skill and co-operation: the companionship of plotters and schemers, of merry talk and informality. And with it all it happened that His

---

December 10th, 1929   WOODBASTWICK   *Ranworth Broad*

84	mallard	Harry Cator, Tim Birkin, Colin McLean, Harry Brown
1	wigeon	and myself
3	shoveler	
7	teal	Morning flight. Fine, S.W. wind. Not so many duck as
1	pintail	expected.
11	pigeons	
1	various	

108

Majesty joined the greatest wildfowler team of all time, a legendary group whose exploits in the 'twenties and early 'thirties will never be surpassed. Possessed of boundless energy, enthusiasm and experience, this intrepid band of Norfolkmen—worthy successors to Hawker, Chapman and Payne-Gallwey, whose hearts they would have gladdened—was invariably in the right place at the right time; if rough weather blew up over Cley and Blakeney they would be there squatting in the marsh; if the wind was west with a touch of north in it they would be up before the first glow in the eastern sky at Ranworth; if ice and snow squalls threatened they would be out after the diving ducks at Hickling. At any moment to any corner of Britain the signal would go out and within hours the team would be assembled in the early darkness ready to disperse to their positions in the reed-beds. In this company His Majesty was immediately at home—he joined, as they had done, the ranks of the great among wildfowler sportsmen; he became, like Hawker, one of the 'fathers of wildfowl shooting'. In this company he was, though a future sovereign, an equal partner in the team.

In 1932 His Majesty was again at Ranworth when six guns got 130 duck and teal at the evening flight, and all the while every season there were constant interludes by Warren Pond and Forfar Loch at Glamis, on a smaller scale, perhaps, but stirring occasions none the less which steadily extended his knowledge and experience of wildfowling. Had they been contemporaries, it would certainly not have been of our King that Payne-Gallwey was thinking when he wrote, 'If a fowler be a rich amateur and desire

August 2nd, 1932	WOODBASTWICK	*Creeks* and *Ranworth Flood*
1 (1) snipe	Harry Cator, Tim Birkin, Oliver Birkbeck, Roger Coke,
117 wild duck	Michael Lyon and myself
13 teal	
3 pigeons	An afternoon and evening flight.
6 various	

140

to shoot fowl, he should set about it in a proper way. If he only wants to frighten the birds for the sake of obtaining two or three a day, he had better remain at home.'

King George the Fifth died in January 1936, and by 1937 the royal shoots were wholly at the disposal of King George the Sixth. It was in this first season of 1937 that a revolution took place at Sandringham. The contrast between the years before his accession and after could not have been more pronounced. Before, as we have seen, no duck was ever shot on flight whilst many hundreds were shot on game shoots. But in 1937 only *41 mallard* were shot during game shoots; yet the season's total at Sandringham was 499 mallard, 53 teal, 1 wigeon, 8 shoveller, 1 gadwall and 5 pintail. And so, in the first season that the King exercised full authority over the royal shooting, of 567 duck recorded at Sandringham 526 were shot *on flight*, and only 41 during ordinary shooting parties.

At last all the pent-up enthusiasm and instinct was released. The deep understanding and love of the wild, which for so many years had been fostered and kindled by Glamis, were given full rein. All the knowledge and experience gained could now be applied to greater potentialities. Sandringham was recognised at once as a wildfowling factor, the pools and marshes were adapted immediately for evening or morning flights. And one evening during the first flighting season at Sandringham the King, stationed at Wolferton Splash, picked over 80 duck to his own gun. And that score, for a single gun, was surely worth more than all the duck that had ever been bagged at Sandringham before.

August 13th, 1937   GLAMIS   *Warren Pond* and *Forfar Loch*
1   rabbit   Michael, David, John, Timothy Lyon and myself
14 (5) snipe
33   wild duck
13   teal   Morning and evening flights. John and Timothy at the
1   various   loch. Dull and damp.
—
62
—

V

DUCK SHOOTING AT SANDRINGHAM

'There are plenty of duck in now' was a message which His Majesty often received in London. It would be a part of the monthly report from Sandringham, and how frequently the King must have wished he could depart at a moment's notice for the precincts of the Wash. Perhaps the weather would be rough in London, and beyond the palace walls the willows in the park would sway with the wind over the sparkling waters of King Charles's lagoon. The wood-pigeons would flight to the parks and squares in the late afternoon, and the mallard quack harshly in restless company as the feeding-hour approached. As the light faded and the traffic lights began to twinkle in the Mall teams of duck would circle above the trees and hurry out beyond the palace grounds to suburban feeding-grounds, silhouetted as they went against the rose-pink glow of London's evening sky. From his window His Majesty would sometimes see them, as he dealt with his papers, and momentarily his mind would have pictured other duck in Norfolk, against a wilder sky on the marshes; he would have thought of his dog, and of his men watching the duck on the ponds and pools, and hoping for his coming. And he would have looked forward eagerly, as we do to our own holidays, to his next trip home and to his next sight of his flight ponds.

In 1937 the King had printed for his use a second game book, specifically for the records of duck-shooting at Sandringham. This is a most beautiful little book, in which a whole page is allotted to a single flight. Down the left-hand side are printed the names of the flighting places; across the top the species of fowl. Thus the names of the participants could be entered against the places where they stood, and the bags at each flight pond could be recorded separately. In this way the King was able to observe how each place improved or otherwise, which species were most inclined to visit each of them, and during which months of the year. This is a rare refinement of wildfowling, and any devotee will appreciate the joy to the author of such specific records.

Earlier in this book, describing the larger volume, it was held that this was sufficient to meet every sportsman's needs, but it was not enough to please the King's eye once Sandringham had been established as a flighting centre. The duck bags were still entered in the main game book, but in it they are only a small feature in the broad pattern of the shooting year. They are, as it were, no more than a single teal would be in a congested ornithological panorama by Hondecoete. When the King wished to compare a flight of one season with that of preceeding years he would have to search back several pages to discover them, and even then he would not be able to remember accurately what proportion of the bag had been shot on, say, Wolferton Splash or Babingley Flat. It was desirable therefore, in view of the various efforts which were put into the development of these places, to have a separate picture of the activity on each. Rather than a small corner of a Hondecoete, the King wanted a whole 'Peter Scott'.[1]

Another factor which prompted the King to devise a more specialised game book was his new interest in duck themselves. The great majority of people who shoot are content to think that

[1] It will be noticed that the King's entries in the duck book are formal by comparison with those in his main book. The reason is probably that his original book was for his own personal records, whereas the duck book was intended to be an official estate register.

October 28th, 1937   Morning flight

48	mallard	*Frankfort Pool:* H. M. the King
2	teal	
1	wigeon	Fine and calm, slight wind. 6.0–7.0 a.m.
1	various	
—		Duck came in steadily in small lots. One lot of 150 teal.
52		

ROYAL WILDFOWLER
*The King about to go out on the
Broad at Hickling*

WOLFERTON
SPLASH

*the foreground is Edward
odd, who took over as head
eper at Sandringham from
Alfred Amos in 1951*

RANWORTH FLOOD

FRANKFORT POND

they have shot so many wild duck and teal. 'Wild duck' is applied
to almost any species that is not a teal, and in its turn teal may
equally well be garganey.[1] In the good old days the 'fathers' were
more specific; 'to the ordinary game-shooter a wild goose repre-
sents the whole group; a wild duck is often similarly classed;
a swan is nothing but a swan and there's an end of it; and a plover
whether green, golden or grey, is simply a plover and good to eat.
But the poorest wildfowler knows better than this, for has he not
shot at least five if not six kinds of wild geese? He can also tell you
that what with one duck and another he recognises at least a
dozen, and has shot them too!'[2] His Majesty did not shoot many
wild geese of any kind,[3] which in these days is a proper example
for all, but he could certainly, 'what with one duck and another',
not only recognise at least a dozen, but had bagged as much
in the storm and the gloaming. The shot who is also a naturalist,
and the wildfowling specialist, is never content with generalities
such as 'duck' and 'teal', and the King appreciated that without

[1] Garganey are now protected under the new Act.

[2] Sir R. Payne-Gallwey, *Letters to Young Shooters.*

[3] The King only shot two wild geese in his life, both pinkfeet, on the
morning of November 13th, 1933, at Kettelshire with Lord Elphinstone.
The morning's bag was 1 wild duck, 1 wigeon and 3 geese, and in his game
book the King wrote: 'a wonderful experience first to hear and then to see
the geese. About 1,000 came in in one lot, and I shot 2. They landed on
the water and then made a terrific noise rising from it.'

November 1st, 1937   Morning flight

111	mallard	*Wolferton Creek:* Earl of Eldon
13	teal	W. A. Fellowes
1	pigeon	*Frankfort Pool:* H. Cator
—		*Park Ponds:* H.M. the King
125		Hon. W. Piers Legh
—		R. S. Demetriadi

Misty and damp. No wind. 6.0–8.0 a.m.

The guns were too close.

disfiguring his main game book, and with the opportunities of varied duck bags which were now open to him, he could not do justice to the records. He was most particular about the classification of species, and he communicated the need for this exactness to those who looked after the duck haunts for him. Duck recognition was strongly encouraged, and coloured illustrations of different ducks were hung in the estate office at Sandringham and in the head keeper's house. And invariably, during his absence from Norfolk, regular reports were despatched to London describing which duck were coming in, and in what numbers. It was the routine for the watchers to lie up by the morning flight pools with binoculars and to make a quiet count of what they could see.

The duck book, therefore, brought a completeness to the new Sandringham innovations. It allowed the great game book to remain a complete record without its neatness being sacrificed for the sake of accuracy, whilst specific details could be confined to the duck book. Thus a morning flight on January 1st, 1938, at Wolferton Creek yielded, according to the main book, 43 wild duck and 6 teal. The same bag in the duck book, however, gives the bag as 34 mallard, 6 teal, 5 shoveler, 1 gadwall and 3 pintail. Both contain tidy entries in the spaces provided, and no crossings-out or amendments were necessary.

Behind the names of the ten places listed down the left-hand margin of each page lies a story of much careful preparation and enterprise. During 1937 the existing ponds and pools were tidied up, reeds and weed cut out where necessary, small platforms piled up for the duck, and shooting tubs, reed hides or screens sited for alternative winds. Certain places were by their nature morning

---

October 27th, 1937   Evening flight
69   mallard   *Wolferton Splash:* H.M. the King
4   teal   W. A. Fellowes
—   *Babingley Flat:* Hon. W. Piers Legh
73   Very wet and dark. Strong S.W. wind. 3.30–5.0 p.m.
—   It is a one-gun place. We were too close together. But
                   duck came in well.

places, and these were made attractive by improving shelter and widening, where possible, the area of clear water.

The morning flights at Sandringham, by contrast with certain other East Anglian reserves, were not notable for very heavy bags. But one would hardly expect otherwise, for the property is not, after all, a broad or a mere, or a vast expanse of swamp and reeds. It is a well-balanced agricultural estate on which there are situated, as on most other estates, a series of ponds. With this in mind, the success of the morning flights which took place is indeed most noteworthy, and old lessons, so often ignored, are handsomely borne out in these records.

When the available water space at Sandringham was surveyed in 1937 from the flighting viewpoint, two pools in the park were scheduled as morning places; also York Cottage Pool, and in the woods there was Donkey Pond and Frankfort. Nearer the Wash there were Boathouse Creek and Pooley's Pond. Now from the outset the primary axiom was observed, that for a successful morning flight the particular locality must forever be undisturbed. A small morning flight place can be upset by simply putting up the fowl in the daytime, and if this is repeated, or done frequently, the duck will soon grow weary of it and rest elsewhere.

Duck are nocturnal in their feeding habits, and all they ask at dawn is to alight on quiet and peaceful waters and after a wash and brush up to sleep soundly, their heads tucked into their backs in happy oblivion. That is why they like great expanses of water where they can relax peacefully in the middle, unconcerned by goings-on on the banks. But they appreciate just as much a secluded pond, sheltered by reeds and trees from the draught, *provided* they are not liable to suffer a violent surprise at close

---

January 1st, 1938   Evening flight
16   mallard   *Wolferton Splash:* H.M. the King
Babingley Flat: H.R.H. the Duke of Gloucester

Dark and wet. N.E. wind. 4.30–4.50 p.m.

Duck came in very late. Too dark to shoot.

quarters and be despatched with startled quacking to renew elsewhere their broken sleep. Duck very soon gain confidence in a
place if they are left alone, but they lose it equally quickly if
they are often alarmed. The most remarkable proof of this is to
be found at Holkham, where the great lake has for generations
been a haven and a sanctuary. Here wild wigeon from the north
pass the winter, and every evening on the coastal flats and
saltings, to which they flight to feed, they are greeted by an
indiscriminate fusillade by all and sundry and peppered at extreme
range; here they are as wild as any wigeon can be. At dawn they
cross inland over the park wall once more and plane down on to
the rippled waters a few steps from the house itself—and then you
can walk to within a few feet of them as they rest a short distance
from the bank or graze on the parkland itself. They are tamer
there than any wild wigeon could be expected to be. This is, of
course, an extreme case; not one generation of wigeon only has
gained confidence in the place, it is an hereditary comprehension.
But it is possible none the less to impart this sense of security in
some degree during the span of one season. A few miles eastwards
from Holkham, at Bayfield, Roger Coke decided not long ago 'to
leave the duck alone'. To-day, on a smaller scale, the ornithological setting is not unmindful of Holkham, and a fine pack of
wigeon and teal carpet the silver reaches all the winter in the
valley of the park.

If, then, the necessary prerequisites can be achieved, pondside
peace and a total absence of daytime interference, all else that is
required is a decent restraint in shooting. And how seldom this is
exercised! At all events Sandringham in His Majesty's day was
exemplary, and in twelve years the King had on his best pool but
sixteen flights. His duties did not permit him to shoot whenever
he wished and he was only able to flight during his spells of holiday at Sandringham, but he never battered his flighting ponds
while he was there. Indeed he had but one, and occasionally two
flights, at any one place during the whole season. After a successful morning flight his enthusiasm did *not* impel him to have
another go a few days later. This would have spoilt the pool. In-

stead he shot it again after a month, if he was still on holiday, and then only if conditions were right. The result was that the morning flight bags were exceptionally consistent.

Frankfort Pond was the place of choice, to which His Majesty invariably went on his own, whilst his guests were distributed at other points. The best bag he ever secured at Frankfort at dawn was 73 duck—*and the lowest 24.* Twenty-four duck at a morning flight is for any of us a worth-while interlude, and Frankfort never yielded the King less than that. But remember once more, sixteen flights at Frankfort in twelve years—that was the secret. The sixteen bags were 52, 48, 25, 37, 47, 54, 26, 31, 49, 36, 43, 56, 44, 73, 24 and 40. What a record! An average of over 40 on a small pond. And this was achieved by the zealous observance of but two criteria, which any man has it in his power to provide— peace and restraint.

Frankfort, through wildfowling eyes, is an unlikely sort of place—but the conventional composition so religiously portrayed of a flat horizon, an extended mirror of water reflecting a bunch of fowl 'coming in' or 'going out', and a speckled or 'mackerel' sky tinted rose or turquoise according to the hour of the clock (most agreeable though this picture may be for the adornment of dressing- or cloak-room), is by no means an essential prerequisite of an authentic bag inland. Duck come for food or rest to strange places—at Holkham mallard flight in the evening into a circular concrete reservoir only ten yards across, and when two hundred ducks are there at night it is certain that you would not see any water at all, but only the backs of the duck. At another

January 15th, 1938   Morning flight
14 mallard   *Wolferton Creek:* H.M. the King
23 teal   Hon. David Bowes-Lyon
 3 shoveler
 1 pigeon   S.W. gale. 6.45–8.0 a.m.
 1 various
——   South end was good. Mallard very chary, but a lot of teal
42   came in.
——

place in the Home Counties an evening flight of lesser proportions was developed underneath a main-line railway viaduct, and sometimes the silver underparts of the last approaching duck were floodlit by the expresses as they thundered past overhead. Not long ago duck flighted to the centre pitch at Lord's when three days' rain prevented the opening of a Test match.

In daylight duck rest happily in London parks and on reservoirs, canals and drains, and in the country as a rule they resort to open water, or small ponds securely masked by a dense fringe of reeds. At Frankfort, however, but a few minutes' flying from the Wash, they rest on a pond in the most ornamental setting imaginable, in the midst of Douglas fir and pine trees and massed banks of rhododendron, round a decorative island approached by a neat bridge in a landscape which might have earned the critical acknowledgment of Capability Brown or Repton. Across this bridge in the early darkness stepped His Majesty, to take up position in one of the tubs sunk on the island. And into this ornamental waterscape flighted the coastal fowl of Norfolk, even though as they swept in they may have been reminded of Virginia Water and the Hog's Back. It has to be owned that there is a distinct stamp of Surrey about this particular part of Norfolk.

On closer study, however, the locality is revealed in a different light, for it possesses character of most ancient fascination. Largely untouched and unscarred since long before the first Romans explored northwards and found themselves halted before a glistening seaboard of creeks and saltings crowning East Anglia, its fauna and flora has changed but little. Over the sandy heathland, the bracken and the heather, the shrill wailing of stone-curlews breaks the stillness of summer nights; the churring of a nightjar

---

January 30th, 1939   Morning flight
  1 mallard   *Wolferton Creek:* Cmdr. H. G. Campbell
  3 teal   *Rix's Creek:* H. M. the King

---

  4   Fine, clear and cold. 7.0–7.20 a.m.
  —   The duck had left the coast. Occupied a new butt.

and the sweet fluting of a woodlark are endemic accompaniments to the murmur of the sea breeze in the top of a lonely pine. These sounds have always been, through countless ages. More often in the past, dotterel on migration ran twittering over the moss, and this open breckland was probably the last nesting stronghold of the great bustard, a specimen of which was not only 'kylled with ye crossbowe on Wedynsday' in 1527, but again in 1838, when the solemn corpse, like a great buff and chestnut Christmas bird, was despatched to the market in Cambridge. Happily, for the sake of tradition and perpetuity, a Constabulary Almanac of 1930 records that on September 1st 'bustard shooting begins' and on March 1st 'bustard shooting ends', but if any old eccentric with a flint-lock muzzle-loader still reveres these august anniversaries, it is perhaps just as well that this fine and handsome quarry no longer 'offers'.[1]

In this seemingly arid land there is plenty of water in the subsoil, and this has led to the creation of many ponds on the 'moors'. Were they in true Surrey they would claim the acquaintance of perhaps only an occasional mallard and a few tufted duck, but being in West Norfolk they enjoy the patronage of all the society of the Wash, from wigeon and golden-eye to curlew and golden plover. And from the river valleys and fens inland come gadwall and garganey, shoveler and snipe. And so these Sandringham ponds, in spite of their unconventional appearance, have the best of all worlds and are popular haunts of all the wildfowl of the county and its coastline, especially in the ideal conditions in which they were maintained by the King.

If morning flight ponds require little else than peace and quiet, on evening places there is always more work to be done and continued attention is demanded. The tubs must be more carefully sited to allow for shooting in a worsening light, and background particularly may have to be demolished to allow the duck to be seen against the sky. During the season daily feeding is necessary, and in this connection the depth of the water is all important, and

---

[1] A Norfolk expression coined in Broadland by Jim Vincent, to describe the arrival or otherwise of duck.

some form of regulation is of immense benefit. Several places were selected as potential evening flight pools, but of them all none proved more successful than Wolferton Splash.

It is geographical location which makes an evening flight pond, and in this respect Wolferton Splash is especially favoured. It is within sound of a gunshot from the marshes and the Wash, and within a mile or two of the morning flight places, and so all about rest duck in quantity. Prospects of an evening flight are not conditioned by whether a likely looking pool is available, but by whether there is a reservoir of fowl within a reasonable distance to be drawn in, and if there are duck somewhere in the area a few might be lured at dusk even to a goldfish pond in the garden.

Wolferton Splash is ideally situated in this respect, but it is no ancient landmark, and the King was indebted for its existence to a German airman, who first excavated a depression by releasing a bomb from a Zeppelin in the First World War. After it filled up with water, duck always frequented it casually, but its true potential was not recognised until 1937. Thereupon it was dug round and broadened, and an island constructed in the centre. Two shooting tubs were sunk. Best of all, a sluice was built so that the water was always kept fresh as well as at the right depth. The result was a classical example of the ideal evening flight pool.

But again it is the last thing in wildfowling haunts which the student of the subject would expect to find alongside the desolate flats of the Wash. The best approach to a good view of it is across 'the moors', through knee-deep heather over which long- and short-eared owls prowl in lazy silence, and where busy parties of

---

October 15th, 1945   Morning flight

93	mallard	*Frankfort Pool:* H.M. the King
8	teal	*Pooley's Pond:* Hon. W. P. Legh
2	shoveler	Viscount Coke
5	pintail	
2	pigeon	*Park Ponds:* Capt. W. A. Fellowes
—		Misty and still. No wind. 5.15–6.45 a.m.
110		
—		Duck came in at fair intervals. Light was good.

crossbills and goldcrests work their restless way through the pines and larches. Then all at once you find yourself on the edge of an escarpment, below which the 'foothills' fall away abruptly to the water meadows; and far beyond is the sea-wall, and then the saltings and the sea. And as you halt on the summit of this promontory there, 100 feet below you, is Wolferton Splash, pear-shaped in the bracken and the heather, and as different in character from the duck haunts of literature and art gallery as can be imagined. And, to bedevil the picture yet further, there just beyond the pool, within three hundred yards, is the main coastal railway, with its 'Emett' express puffing northwards over its bleak unsheltered course until, like the Romans, it is constrained to halt by the North Sea.

But duck, unlike their slayers, are not martyrs to taste or convention, and one pool is as good as another to them, provided they have peace, food and fresh water, and the water at a nice depth so that they can stand on their heads and reach the bottom. The Splash has it all, and whether it is Surrey or the North Riding that the flighting duck is reminded of as he swishes in to settle by the island, he soon forgets these reflections as he finds a good meal with staccato chuckling in the last light of day.

The first flight which ever took place at the Splash was on the evening of October 27th, 1937. The King went there with a companion, whilst a third gun went to Babingley Flat. At the Splash the new tubs were occupied, but the wind was blowing directly from one to the other. The King was downwind and had the

---

October 11th, 1947   Morning flight

122	mallard	*Frankfort Pool:* H.M. the King
3	teal	*Donkey Pond:* Capt. W. A. Fellowes
2	wigeon	*Park Ponds:* Viscount Coke
4	shoveler	*York Cottage Pond:* Major M. Adeane
4	pintail	
2	pigeon	Fine and still. No wind. 6.30–7.15 a.m.

---

137   Duck came in well. There was one big lot of mallard.

chance of a very good shoot, but he left a great many duck so that they might go through to the rear gun, who in his turn and with equal consideration left a proportion of these which were more aloft in the hope that they would wheel round again over the King. Inevitably a great many settled without being shot at. Nevertheless, as a trial of a new place, they must have been much encouraged, since there was a fine show of duck and they picked up 47 mallard and 4 teal. At Babingley 22 mallard were collected.

The King's companion was, however, convinced that the Splash could accommodate only one gun, and persuaded the King that this was the case. His Majesty remarked in his duck book, 'It is a one-gun place', and thereafter he went there alone.

The next evening flight was on November 25th. A nice lot of duck had been watched in on previous evenings, and as there was a fresh south wind hopes ran high. The King again went to Wolferton Splash, this time on his own, and two guns to Babingley Flat. Mallard streamed in in small parties during the early evening and until dusk, and the King had a superb flight. He picked up 80 mallard and 1 pintail himself. This is a memorable single-gun bag at an evening flight at any time and has not often been surpassed. The rest of the party got 21 mallard and 4 teal, making a total bag of 106 duck. The King described it as 'the greatest fun'.

One can well imagine the fine sensation which this spectacular event must have occasioned the King and those who had assisted him to introduce flighting at Sandringham. It was an early and crowning triumph for all their thought and effort. It is also a wonderful example of what can be done by the intelligent application of wildfowling lore. Before that season no duck had ever

---

November 25th, 1937   Evening flight

101	mallard	*Wolferton Splash:* H.M. the King
4	teal	*Babingley Flat:* A. F. Lascelles
1	pintail	W. A. Fellowes
—		Fine. South wind. 3.0–5.0 p.m.
106		
—		A very good flight. Duck came in steadily in small lots.

been flighted at Sandringham. At the second attempt one man killed eighty-one to his own gun. However exceptional the marksmanship of His Majesty, the presentation of a sufficient number of duck to afford such a bag was a most singular achievement in itself.

Though the morning flighting was so consistent, it must not be thought that the King never had a disappointing experience. If this was true he could hardly have been an experienced wild-fowler, for one would learn very little if on every occasion there was an agreeable plethora of birds. Evening flights are, as a rule, more chancy, because so often the wind particularly cannot be depended upon. In Norfolk it has a peculiar and exasperating habit of blowing well all day, so that one decides to flight, and then dropping flat as the sun sinks, thus making one wish one had not ventured forth. Nothing can be worse than a calm evening, since gunshots, sounding in the stillness like the thumpings of Big Bertha, seem to thunder and reverberate round the district and cause instant reaction among the incoming duck. In the evening the flight is much more concentrated, limited, except for occasional early visitations and very late stragglers, to perhaps half an hour. Thus every shot is liable to drive off birds which are near at hand and on the way, and these in turn wheel off in alarm and spread apprehension among those further behind which they pass. Often in these circumstances the flighter is in the miserable predicament when he is crouching below a circling company of various duck parties, hesitating to shoot just one bird and thus banish all the rest.

This could happen to the King as much as to anyone else, as could all other perversities of wildfowl which can never be predicted. After another flight at the Splash in 1938, when he got only 15 mallard, he remarked in his book, 'Duck came in very late. Too dark to shoot.' A month later he again flighted the Splash— and killed 2 duck. He was in the same tub where, two months earlier, he had picked up eighty-one. Both these bags are records in their different ways for Wolferton Splash, and after the 'two' he remarked, 'Duck came in in the dark and settled out of shot.'

The other gun, who was at Babingley, wrote in his game book, 'Duck settled out of shot, and came in in the dark.' So now we know the story.

The King had as well, like the rest of us, unexplained disappointments. There was no evening flighting at Sandringham after the outbreak of war, since the pools were not fed, and the first visit to Wolferton Splash after 1939 was in 1948. On an October evening he went back once more to the old tub which had served him so well, and killed only 11 mallard. In his book he wrote, 'We have started up this place again. Over 100 duck were counted in on the nights before. Very few arrived, and it was nearly dark.'

The King was always looking for possibilities of improvement whenever he was shooting, and recorded his impressions in his game book. After one flight he notes, 'A barrel instead of a butt will improve vision.' After another, 'Duck difficult to see. Fences to be cut down.' Later, after he had made a recommendation for Pooley's Pond, he wrote after a flight, 'Duck came in well. Removal of bushes a great improvement.'

Perhaps by now the reader may be thinking that this book, which has as its subject a game book largely recording royal bags of grouse, partridges and pheasants, awards undue prominence to the King's more infrequent excursions at flight-time. But one of his friends, who saw as much of him in the shooting field as any, once wrote: 'I really think he was more fond of duck-shooting than anything else, and I think he was, if anything, better at shooting duck than any other game.' If duck-shooting is the cream of sport with the shotgun, and if, as we know, His Majesty attained the highest refinement and accomplishment in that sport,

---

October 17th, 1949   Evening flight
  9   mallard   *Wolferton Splash:* H.M. the King
  4   teal
  —   Fine and mild. S.W. wind. 6.30–7.10 p.m.
 13
  —   Very few duck came in.

then surely that friend was right. Thus we may be forgiven for dwelling on this particular aspect.

The sad fact is, however, that the King, though he was able to fire his gun to the last, was prevented through ill health from flighting after 1949. Wildfowling is a Spartan game, and it is always foolhardy to run risks in the cold dampness of a winter's dawn or the sudden chill of evening. Thus the last duck flight which the King ever enjoyed at Sandringham was on the morning of October 18th, 1949. But we may rejoice that it was a success. He had with him a large party of his relations and closest friends. The seven of them were disposed from Wolferton Creek and Pooley's to the Park Ponds, York Cottage Pool and Donkey Pond. The King, as usual, was at Frankfort. It was as if by chance the whole cast was brought in and all the scenic apparatus brought into play for the final act. There was a strong south-west wind, it was wet and dark—ideal conditions for a morning flight. There were not an exceptional number of duck about at that time, and the King notes as well that they were 'rather chary'. Nevertheless it was a good morning by any standards and the total bag was 54 mallard, 43 teal, 7 wigeon, 3 shoveler, 4 gadwall, 1 pintail, 1 pigeon—a total of 113 head. The King, shooting alone at his favourite Frankfort Pool, picked 23 mallard, 10 teal, 1 wigeon, 1 shoveler, 4 gadwall and 1 pintail, a total of 40 duck—happily almost the exact average of all the bags he had ever obtained at

---

October 18th, 1949   Morning flight

54	mallard	*Wolferton Creek:* Major M. Adeane
43	teal	Capt. W. A. Fellowes
7	wigeon	*Frankfort Pool:* H.M. the King
3	shoveler	*Deershed Pool:* H.R.H. Duke of Gloucester
4	gadwall	*Park Ponds:* Hon. David Bowes-Lyon
1	pintail	*York Cottage Pond:* Hon. Michael Bowes-Lyon
1	pigeon	*Donkey Pond:* Lt.-Col. Hon. Sir Piers Legh

113   Wet and dark. Strong S.W. wind. 6.45–7.30 a.m.

Quite a lot of duck came in large lots. Rather chary.

Frankfort. And so, on the last occasion when the King rose eagerly in the early darkness at Sandringham in quest of duck, he had an excellent morning flight.

So much may be learned from the game book. But what is not recorded is that this flight, as well as being the King's last, was the first ever watched by Princess Elizabeth. Well wrapped up, with a scarf about her head, she crossed in the darkness to the island on Frankfort Pond; in the silence father and daughter waited together before the first light of dawn.

If continuity is a precious feature of our heritage, then there is poignancy in the thought that here, in the depths of England, George the Sixth was out after the fowl before sunrise, while Elizabeth the Second crouched by him to see how these things should be done.

VI

SUMMER HOLIDAY

We are indeed most fortunate to be able to learn of the King's life in Scotland from the recollection of an anonymous contributor who was a guest at Balmoral each year from the time of His Majesty's accession. To the reader this separate viewpoint on the King as a shot will come as a refreshing interlude, and we are much in debt for so personal and engaging a contribution on the life which he enjoyed at his Scottish home.

Our contributor writes:

A personal memoir, designed to recall the experiences and tastes in shooting of the person commemorated, exposes the author to a task of peculiar difficulty, even when he has access to game books as complete and accurate as the King's, for these, however valuable for purposes of record, are apt to be tantalising for what they omit rather than illuminating for what they disclose.

Only one thing is certain, that the biggest days are rarely those which brought the greatest pleasure.

What were the characteristics, then, which brought to the King the immense enjoyment which shooting gave to him?

There was, I think, no single factor, but a great variety of attendant delights, each making its contribution to a pleasure which in his case certainly—for he was the most companionable of shooters—relied fundamentally upon the sharing of his pastimes with his friends.

Marksmanship certainly was one element, and always must be. Who can recall without a modest happiness those magic days when no pheasant was too high and no grouse too fast, and when one's dog found a succession of runners (one's neighbours', of course) with unfailing brilliance.

By some blessed contrivance they remain in one's mind, fresh and precise, long after one has forgotten those dark occasions when one could hit nothing, when one's dog ran in twice, and when sent across a stream to collect a woodcock on the other side (one's solitary token of competence), would only poke about in the reeds after moorhens.

The King was a most beautiful shot. I have seen him kill high grouse coming downwind, one after another and all as dead as doornails, with a skill which could stand any comparison.

He derived, I think, infinite satisfaction (as most people do) from the performance of what he did well, and this zest found him always equally eager, whether he had drawn the best place in a good partridge drive, or was shooting a few rabbits at Sandringham when pheasant shooting was finished.

It is common to see birds of no great quality missed by competent shots because they are really indifferent to the result, but that was never the King's way.

He devoted a complete attention to everything which came within his range, and it was this, I think, which made him so effective a shot.

He early abandoned any tradition whereby the King at every stand had the best place, and though he had a few favourite spots, endeared to him by long familiarity, he habitually shared alike with his friends.

Another of his contributing pleasures lay in the setting: the wide winter fields of West Norfolk, brown and russet after Christmas frost, and spanned by a great arc of blue sky; or the

---

August 15th, 1924   STUDLEY ROYAL   *Tom's Corner*
  3 snipe   Clare Vyner, Michael Lyon and myself
185 grouse
———   Fine day with a strong wind. Birds came very well indeed.
188
———

THE KING IN THE HIGHLANDS

LOCH MUICK

After a picnic the party drags the edge of the loch for small trout. With the King are the Master of Elphinstone and Lord Salisbury

BALMORAL

The King and Queen during a day of sunshine on the hill

hillside at Balmoral as the guns one after another filed into their allotted butts, each taking stock of a view which for all its familiarity is ever new—the far skyline shimmering in the distance, and three or four grouse, put up by the outgoing flankers, swinging diagonally across the line, well out of shot.

Lastly, and perhaps most valued, the companionship of well-tried friends, drawn together not by any thought of competition but by the common sharing of a pleasure which brought an unlimited happiness to all.

There was no more kind or generous host than the King, and he used, I think, to prefer what was familiar to what was new, both in persons and in places.

His extraordinary memory invested every corner with some recollection, not always of the most flattering order, nor the better for being, invariably, scrupulously accurate.

'Do you remember being fast asleep when a snipe came over you here?'

'No, Sir, certainly not.'

Vain protest, as all knew.

I remember that years ago when we were shooting on the hill called 'The Brown Cow' I ventured upon a mildly regrettable pun. Forever after, whenever we passed this feature (as one does whenever approaching Corndavon), the King would say to me, 'Do you remember that frightful joke you made about The Brown Cow?'

Self, with emphatic innocence, 'No, Sir.'

'Oh yes you do; you said . . .' and out would come the patient skeleton, rattling its unrespectable bones, to the sour glee of the other occupants of the shooting bus.

August 15th, 1935 GANNOCHY

1,022 grouse	Mr. J. P. Morgan, Sidney E., Hampden, H. Morgan,
1 various	David L., Arthur Penn, John E. and myself
————	Fine S. breeze, masses of birds. I shot 84 birds in No. 5
1,023	butt. 233 brace big drive. A wonderful day.

These recollections seem trifling enough as I read them through, but I think they may serve to strike a chord in the memory of those who were devoted to His Majesty, and maybe they will take comfort, as I do myself, from the thought that it was against a background which I have tried to depict that the King spent his last days—not as a weary invalid condemned to a sick-bed, but as one who had, as he believed, conquered his tribulations, after being able once again to see to an end a shooting season in which, in its latter days, he could play a full and happy part.

.   .   .   .   .   .

To his home at Balmoral, I think, the King set off with greater zest than to any other. For one thing its welcome came at a time when, above all others, it was most appreciated: it seemed to offer a reward for many months of unceasing engagements, and for weeks before the departure from London really arrived, release must have danced entrancingly before the imagination of all those to whom it had for so long beckoned.

For years I used to foregather, in early August, with other members of the household, in the garden entrance of Buckingham Palace, to wish Their Majesties godspeed, and it was an unfailing pleasure, for an atmosphere of delight and excitement enveloped us all.

As we waited, gossiping cheerfully to each other, bustling heralds of departure would pass continually to the waiting cars, footmen carrying small despatch cases, and—inexplicably—endless pairs of shoes: others with leather satchels containing magazines and papers, and stuffed with those letters to which a reply

---

August 22nd, 1938 BALMORAL *Gairnshiel*
 4 hares   Jack Eldon, Cranborne, David Lyon, Arthur Penn, Joey
450 grouse   Legh, Ross and myself.

---

454   Fine and still. We saw a lot of birds.

had long been deferred in the fragile hope that there would be plenty of time for a really undisturbed consideration at Balmoral.

Then at last, from the descending lift, first a cascade of dogs, making themselves, if possible, more easily heard than usual, then the Princesses, dancing down the steps, and behind them the King and Queen, radiating goodwill in the anticipation of their well-earned and lovely holiday.

I see the King saying *au revoir* to each of us separately with a friendliness which seemed to embrace us all within the ambit of his own contentment.

A fundamental difference between Sandringham and Balmoral lay in the history of the latter.

What appealed to Queen Victoria, when she bought it soon after her wedding, seems to have been the contrast it provided with her life of ceremony and routine in London, the simplicity and directness of her Scottish subjects, and the beauty of the surroundings (which repeatedly reminded the Prince Consort of Thuringia).

She delighted in picnics and expeditions of all kinds, and the sport open to the Prince Consort lay in shooting deer: grouse and blackcock enjoyed a very modest place in the list of available diversions.

Even in King George the Fifth's day there was hardly any grouse-driving: for this he used to visit the homes of his friends, at Bolton, Abbeystead, Moy or Floors, and by the time he reached Balmoral stalking was beginning, and formed his chief preoccupation until he came South.

August 19th, 1946 BALMORAL *Tomboddies* and *Blairglass*
12 hares   Philip, Eldon, Cranborne, David L., Althorp and myself
 1 snipe
 1 black game Fine, N.W. wind. Saw a nice lot of young birds.
210 grouse

224

The late King, however, preferred to spend his holidays with his family and his friends, and succeeded in leasing some of the Invercauld moors, first Gairnshiel and, later, Corndavon.

By an extraordinarily happy chance he found available, and within a mile or so of his home, some of the best grouse-driving in Scotland, and at once he set about making the most of his acquisition—new keepers were added, and Gillan, a skilled and untiring general, was put in command.

A programme of heather-burning and drainage was planned, new roads and bridges were gradually developed, and the driving was surveyed with a concentrated attention.

As often, the planning of the last century was as skilful for grouse-driving as it was lamentable for pheasants, and for many drives the butts only needed repair, but a number of new lines were added to suit alternative winds, and many of them—some supremely successful—were based entirely on the King's observation.

His approach to shooting here, therefore, was in direct contrast with his rôle at Sandringham.

There he was in some respects content to follow precedent: here he was the originator, and, as may be supposed, this gave him an overwhelming satisfaction.

Only a few years ago he bought some of the Glenmuick estate, and embarked upon a further innovation, which was to drive grouse on the forests. Although many of his neighbours had long done this, tradition at Balmoral had always regarded such a violation as almost sacrilegious, and this was an innovation indeed.

He himself largely planned the drives, first with experimental butts, which could either be adopted or corrected, in the light of experience.

August 25th, 1947 BALMORAL *Black Hillock* and *Brown Cow*

| 219 | grouse | Philip, David L., Salisbury, Eldon, Stanley, S. Ramsay |
| 1 | various | and myself |

---

220 Fine and hot. More birds than last year.

First trials were encouraging: their successors, which were even better, saw his skilled pioneering triumphantly vindicated, and last year the forest showed more grouse than anywhere else on the estate.

It was no wonder that his Scottish home gave him some of his happiest hours, for it was he who had created its abundance.

I have a vivid picture of shooting mornings, with the guns assembled in the hall, waiting for their host to join them.

Punctual to the minute he would come from his room, where he had already conferred with Gillan as to the day's plans, and also transacted some business, his face already displaying his pleasure at what lay before him.

He always wore his own tweed, which he had devised for himself and his keepers, and for those members of his household who were fortunate enough to be given a length.

In one hand would be a long walking-stick, in the other, very often, some special article of apparel of his own planning for combating any possible trick of the weather: a cap, a scarf, or some ingenious kind of coat, for he was always a great contriver.

We would all clamber into the bus, which at once became full of chatter, and about once a week whoever was nearest the door would lower the window a little, in order to inspire the storm of imprecation which instantly followed an act of such suicidal folly, for the King always unshakeably maintained that the exhaust and the window were fatally conjoined, and always had been.

This and many other familiar features assumed gradually a ritualistic virtue which was widely recognised.

Others were the site of the opening day of the season, before driving really began, a rabbit shoot among the juniper bushes, in a region known as 'Back of Wood', and expeditions on Sunday afternoons either to the far end of Loch Muick, for tea in the Glassalt or some light-hearted trout-fishing in the Loch—or to the Queen's charming little cottage. There a more serious and less reputable form of fishing often produced some salmon, bearing mysterious marks almost suggestive of foul hooking.

On driving days most of the house party joined the guns for

luncheon, which was always in the open. Formerly luncheon used to be deployed and served by footmen, but this was abandoned many years ago.

The luncheon baskets were deposited in some favourite situation, plaid rugs would be spread about the heather and bog-myrtle, and since by one of the most hallowed of shooting conventions the ladies were usually on the spot before the guns had descended from the hillside, they had often already removed from the hampers the delicious contents which nobody who has enjoyed them could ever forget.

In retrospect the sun seems so continuously to have shone on these Lucullan festivals that many would have been understandably content to prolong them almost indefinitely, but the King had ever a watchful eye upon the afternoon's programme, and in due course a busy repacking would begin, rather on the lines of happy families, one collecting plates, another knives and forks, and a third coffee cups, until at last the straps were fastened once again, and a procession, now increased in numbers, would wind diagonally up the hillside to the next drive.

When Land-rovers, after the war, made their valued appearance, a canvas shelter of rather uncertain stability tempered the austerity of wind or rain.

Latterly the King, whose early ardour tempted him to shoot every day of the week, used to dedicate one day to a rest, which gave the keepers and drivers a break, and brought for himself and his guests a chance of catching up with mounting arrears of correspondence.

In a favourable year he used to drive grouse throughout

August 23rd, 1948 BALMORAL *Tomboddies* and *Blairglass*

1	hare	Harry, Philip, David L., Salisbury, Eldon, H. Fraser and
164	grouse	myself
1	various	
—		Showery. S.W. gale spoilt the day. A good last drive at
166		Blairglass.

September and even into October, when the first frost had already begun to dress Deeside in gold and crimson.

So the happy weeks passed, with a succession of guests filling the castle and enjoying a hospitality which surely can have had no equal anywhere else.

It was the King who was the inspiration of it all, and his example and his kindness will long warm the hearts of those who look back.

They will rejoice, too, to think that there remains at Balmoral the memorial which he would most have valued, an unbroken continuation of what he himself created with so much skill, care and love.

. . . . . .

It has been suggested that some record should be made of a day at Balmoral on September 3rd, 1945, not because it was characteristic but for precisely the opposite reason.

It was an indifferent grouse year and by September several beats had been shot hard enough. The castle contained a full team of guns, and it was suggested that instead of further reducing the stock of grouse we might apply ourselves to trying to fill the game card with everything which the resources of Balmoral could provide.

The King may have remembered that many years before, in 1924, a similar project at Invermark had been frustrated by the weather, and then as now, Salisbury, Eldon, David Lyon and I, as well as the King himself, had all been present.

Therefore he eagerly welcomed this proposal and applied himself at once to the arts of generalship and the most effective deployment of his resources. Three small individual parties were

September 7th, 1948 BALMORAL *Rinetton*
1   partridge   M. Adeane and myself
4   hares
103 rabbits   Fine. An afternoon after rabbits. We saw a great many!

108

detailed to pursue victims whose habit led them away from the rest: the remaining guns were charged with the responsibility for the bulk of the task, with liberty to detach lesser units if desirable.

The King himself undertook, with John Elphinstone, to climb Lochnagar in search of ptarmigan. Princess Elizabeth, accompanied by Margaret Elphinstone, was to supply a stag: Jack Eldon was detailed to produce the salmon and trout and took a gun with him: if I remember aright he shot a duck and something not usually appearing on any menu: I think it was either a heron or a hawk.

The day was grilling, and those dedicated to the mountain tops handed out some pretty dirty looks at their less adventurous fellow conspirators: their efforts, however, were triumphant; the King and John shot 6 ptarmigan and several of the grouse, and Princess Elizabeth soon had a stag.

John Elphinstone has written of his expedition with the King, 'After breakfast we set off in one of the Ford brakes. As we got on to the road across the forest, the King, who was in tremendous form, decided that some sport might already be forthcoming, and so we each "manned" a window, one either side, with our guns pointed out. Before long we saw a good covey of grouse gritting on the road ahead, which waited until we were almost on them before they rose. Then they split up, half the covey flying away each side of the car, and directly at right angles to the road. We each fired at our respective half-covey, and, unbelievably, each got two grouse. A very good omen for the day, we thought.

'Arrived at the Glassalt, we started on the steep climb up to the ptarmigan world. It was a cloudless and very hot day, and before

August 18th, 1949 BALMORAL *South Gairn*
  3 black game Philip, David L., Salisbury, Eldon, H. Fraser, R. Camp-
263 grouse bell and myself
  2 golden plover
—— Fine, S.W. wind. Saw more birds to-day.
268

we had gone far we were discarding our coats and ties, and wondering whether we should ever make the top.

'Eventually we reached the jumbled chaos of rocks and stones which runs round the top of the whole Lochnagar massif, and there we lined out—McHardy, the King and Jimmy McGregor, with myself at the top.

'Ptarmigan are curiously unreliable and shifting birds, as we were soon to discover. We jumped, scrambled and balanced precariously over the rocks, and for a long time not a ptarmigan did we see except for three very wild birds which rose two hundred yards ahead and soared away out of sight into the blue.

'Then at last far below me I saw a single ptarmigan rise very far out in front of the King who, with an amazingly good shot, hit it very hard indeed, and the bird fell a long way down the steep slope beyond him. The King set off in gallant pursuit, whilst I sat down lazily, perspiring and exhausted, watching the distant search. Then to my joy I saw the King find his bird. One great objective, a ptarmigan, was secured and had been bagged by the King himself!

'Whilst I sat there in the hot sun watching McHardy and the King climbing back to their places in the line, I suddenly heard somewhere very close the familiar and rather rude guttural croak of a ptarmigan. I looked round and heard it again, and then saw an old ptarmigan very erect on the edge of a rock. It was only twenty yards away, and I made out several more birds crouching about him, nearly invisible against the grey stone. I seized my gun and advanced on the birds, and as they rose I fired at the old bird which had croaked. To my amazement two other birds fell as well, and to complete my astonishment I killed yet two more birds with my left barrel.

'After this unexpected skirmish we did not go much further, but decided to rejoin the rest of the party. We made our way down again, shooting a grouse or two on the homeward walk.

'The King was full of chaff at my lazy method of shooting ptarmigan—"Really! I do all the climbing up and down, and all the hard work, and *you* just sit on a rock and shoot five ptarmigan in two shots without moving a yard!" But be that as it may, it was the King himself who got the one ptarmigan which really mattered, and it was a very fine shot at that.'

The rest of us found our mission full of contradictions. A capercailzie, which might easily have baffled our search, appeared very early: our most severe problems proved to be a pheasant (which, incidentally, should have been entitled to nearly a month's immunity, but being a very rare species at Balmoral, was included) and a woodcock.

We didn't bother much about the woodcock, thinking that it would be readily forthcoming, but it was the last to give in: we had almost given up hope when at last one turned up between the garden and the garage.

Jack Eldon has described the woodcock event, as well as his other experiences which proved to be of major importance in the compilation of the bag.

'I was given the task of getting as many varieties of fish and anything else that I could find. I started in a car with several ladies, and was driven up to the bridge over the Gairn near the Gillie's cottage. I managed to extract two salmon out of the pool above the bridge, but failed to hook a sea trout, although I had caught one in this pool only two days before. I doubt if there were any present, as I gave it a good "raking" with several triangles.

'I then motored up the Gairn to Corndavon Lodge and tried a pool up there which was reputed to be a favourite haunt of sea trout, but except for picking up some scales which I believe came from the back of a salmon I had no luck at all.

'I then attacked the big loch above the lodge, hoping to catch a brown trout and a char. One of the ladies rowed me up and down the loch for about two hours, but I only succeeded in catching a

---

September 14th, 1949   BALMORAL   *Black Hillock* and *South Gairn*

  1   hare   David L., John E., Brabourne, Dalkeith, J. Hope, Tryon
402   grouse   and myself

———

403   Showery, later fine. We got 91 brace in 2nd drive a.m.

———

few small brown trout. The loch itself must have been too cold for the char, as they always lie very deep in cold water, and the evening is the best time to catch them rising. Afterwards we returned to the car and started back for lunch at Balmoral. On the way down I spotted a heron poaching the river in a small pool, and I could not resist stalking him. He gave me an easy shot as he rose, and I shot several grouse as well on the way back. I also had an unsuccessful stalk after a roe on "Tomboddies". We all met for a late luncheon, according to plan.

'It was then found that we were short of mallard and woodcock, so after a glorious picnic on the lawn we lined out and walked the wood east of the castle, towards the lodge. I walked down the road and while I paused to talk to the policeman who was on duty at the crossroads, I suddenly saw a hen capercailzie sitting on top of a fir tree above us. I shot it and it almost landed on his head, and I have never seen a policeman so surprised as he was, particularly as he had never seen a 'caper' before in his life. It had probably been sitting there all the morning looking down at him.

'As we failed to get a woodcock it was decided that we should try a drive at a small loch where there is usually a mallard. We posted ourselves as best we could round the loch and I remember trying rather hopelessly to hide behind a fencing post. There were two or three mallard at home and one gave me a pretty high chance and I managed to get one pellet into his head and down he

---

August 21st, 1950	BALMORAL *Tulloch* and *Rinetton Wood*
5 hares	Philip, Harold C., Plunket and myself
188 rabbits	
2 woodcock	Fine. A rabbit day. Two short grouse drives.
2 snipe	
1 black game	
30 grouse	
1 capercailzie	

229

came. So that was a mallard, but we were still short of a wood-cock.

'The King then decided that the best chance was to drive the fir wood from below the Boat Pool towards Balmoral. Some guns went back, and others were posted in a line from the river towards the castle. By then it was beginning to get rather dark and, if I remember correctly, there were two or possibly three woodcock in the wood. However, only one came forward and gave me an easy shot to my right. But it fell slap into the River Dee, which was in full spate! Everyone ran like mad to get below it, and finally a keeper's dog retrieved the bird to the shore. And so ended a great day.'

On the King's next birthday those who took part gave our host a silver table-mat to stand under his plate. Around his cypher in the centre there were engraved the names of the guns, the date and the bag. It invariably lay before him thereafter, as a reminder of a happy day.

September 3rd, 1945 BALMORAL

1	pheasant	Lilibet (stag), Eldon, Cranborne, David L., A. Penn,
12	partridges	John Elphinstone, Joey L. (roedeer), M. Adeane and
1	mountain hare	myself
1	brown hare	
3	rabbits	A lovely day. Went in small parties to collect the 19
1	woodcock	varieties. John and I shot the ptarmigan on Lochnagar.
1	snipe	
1	wild duck	
1	stag	
1	roedeer	
2	pigeon	
2	black game	
17	grouse	
2	capercailzie	
6	ptarmigan	
2	salmon	
1	trout	(*N.B.*—The 2 various were a heron
2	various	and a sparrow-hawk.)

57

VII

THE KING AS A GUEST

One morning after the war the sweeping landscape of North Norfolk lay tranquil beneath the wide October sky. The early sun was yet too weak to bring a sparkle to the stubbles, but the clouds were high and a faint breeze made the hedgerows vibrant. The broad fields sloped away in harmonious undulation towards the saltings and the sea, where idle breakers lapped the sand-dunes in the far distance. To the west, in the heart of great partridge ground, Nelson's birthplace crouched out of sight by a reed-fringed brook. Northwards on the crest of a coastal rise Overy Mill stood sentinel over the creeks and waterways, and directly to the north the stately belt of trees surrounding Holkham Park stretched to the horizon behind its russet wall.

On a peaceful by-road at the south-west corner of the park a small group was waiting. For many reasons there was an air of expectancy and optimism among those present; for some, simply to stand on a Norfolk upland overlooking the sea on a fine October morning is enough to stir the spirit—the sensation of spacious freedom which the Norfolk scene inspires in the lovers of this land is sufficient in itself to bring contentment and hope. But this was, as well, one of the best shooting days to be had in England, perhaps in the world. This highlight in the shooting year, the first day over the Burnham beat, embodies all the essential prerequisites of the perfect day's shooting. Rural England at peace, its natural beauty unscarred by development; the keen air and the scent of the sea; the smooth timing and skilful operation of the manoeuvres, yet at the same time the atmosphere of informality and merriment, which is lost when the company is too concerned with the size of the bag; the level of accomplishment and comprehension of the party, and the enthusiasm of the host; and lastly, that indefinable atmosphere of simple splendour which neither money nor sophistication can procure, which is born of tradition and continuity, of which the keepers' bowler hats and the ancient game-wagon are only visible symptoms; this last no new ambition can surpass, because it grows up with a place where sport has for generations been an organic part in the living body of a miniature realm. If some other properties may occasionally produce more partridges, they will never afford a day more rich and diverse in enjoyment for the discerning sportsman.

All this, then, was in store for the party on that fine October morning. But there was still one more thing which would lift the day to the stature of memorable occasions, the final brush-stroke to a Norfolk canvas already rich in tone. For the King was to be one of the party, and the little group on the by-road were now awaiting him.

Punctually at the appointed moment the maroon shooting-brake, a familiar spectacle in Norfolk, came into view down the narrow road. When it drew up, the King's companions alighted and stood aside, and then out stepped His Majesty, a trim figure in a Norfolk jacket made of his own cloth, his tweed cap at a jaunty angle. He was a merry monarch on this sunny morning, in high spirits and as eager as any of the party to be on the move. He shook hands with each guest in turn, and then guns and loaders moved briskly on to line the roadside hedge. It was more than a

---

January 4th, 1946   HOLKHAM   *Old Common* and *Scarborough*
301   pheasants   Leicester, Coke, David Lyon, A. Penn, Dick Moly-
3   partridges   neux, T. Harvey, W. Fellowes, S. Van Neck, J. A.
26   hares   Keith and myself
10   rabbits
29 (8) woodcock
5   various   Fine but very cold.

374

privilege to shoot with the King; it was a treat to become infected with the glowing warmth of his obvious relish and eager anticipation. As the party found their pegs and settled into position, the head keeper, his bowler disappearing over the horizon to a flank, blew a wavering blast on his horn. The curtain was up.

The host had placed the guns for the first drive, and the King was No. 6, second from the left. Thereafter everyone moved up two, normally, including His Majesty—he preferred that. In the silent moments after the drive had begun, the breeze freshened into a gentle wind, which the birds would have behind their tails, and soon a covey appeared in front, gliding for the line, but settled 100 yards short. Somewhere ahead a French partridge was calling, and then a distant clamour arose beyond the park as a throng of Canadian geese returned to the lake from their feeding-grounds out on the uplands.

There was one lesson to be learned from the King during the brief spells of waiting. No man could have been more alert. Unless it was certain that no bird approached, and it is difficult to be certain, he was always at the ready; the briefest movement could bring the gun to the shoulder, and in a fraction of a second he could fire. Thus partridges were usually taken in front, as they should be, just as soon as they appear. This expertness, so easily and so often described, is less easy to practise, and even those who preach and write of it do not so frequently demonstrate their convictions. Certainly it is impossible if one is slumped on a shooting-stick with a gun under one's arm. Alertness, awareness and concentration are the fundamentals of good partridge shooting. The King employed them all with sharp enthusiasm.

A cock pheasant sailed for the beech trees at the corner of the park and was killed by the left-hand gun. It fell over the wall, and the first shot of the day had been fired. A few seconds later another cock did the same thing, though gliding lower, with the same result. And then all at once, unexpectedly, the first wave of single Frenchmen broke through the hedge at intervals along the line and, as always, caught some of the guns unawares. But not the King, who killed two as they climbed steeply in front of him after sighting the guns. They whirred upwards, as redlegs often do when the guns are standing back, in suicidal ascent. Surely there is no easier shot, yet how often these birds, by a combination of surprise and perplexingly leisured flight, defeat the most experienced guns. With a calm head, however, there should be no mistake, and the King on this occasion opened his day with a convincing right and left, and then killed a third with the second gun. He was smiling broadly; he was enjoying himself.

The first three drives were devised to collect the partridges into a wide bay of broad fields against the park woodland. At the second drive the guns stood up to a low hedge and the birds were brought uphill so that they topped the hedge at eye-level and scattered among the guns, twisting in all directions behind the line, and some wheeling right round and crossing the line again from behind, climbing off towards the beaters. The line was on the crest of a hill, so that the field behind also sloped sharply away towards the coast, and the birds which continued forwards were always dropping as they whirred on behind the guns.

Such a drive does not conform to the orthodox conception of a good stand, but it is the stand at which you can recognise an outstanding shot. The 'good stand' is not only the most enjoyable and the most satisfying experience, but in some ways, for the experienced shot, the easiest with which to contend. Standing well back from a tall hedge in low ground, with the coveys passing swiftly over at tree-top height, there is no cause for panic or haste, and little likelihood of surprise. It is like playing fast bowling slightly outside the off-stump. If you do not dwell on the bird, or poke, but simply carry out the established technique of a quick, even swing at the appropriate moment, and use your feet and keep your head, as often as not success should attend you. Of course we all lose our heads constantly, and achieve incomprehensible misses, but there is less occasion for them at a 'good stand' than at the one we are now observing.

It is here that the expert reveals himself. Partridges are all around you, at all heights, moving in all directions, approaching from any quarter, some fast, some slow, some climbing, some

HOLKHAM
*The King waiting at Burnham Thorpe before
the first drive over the valley*

SANDRINGHAM

Luncheon behind a haystack during a partridge shoot. With the King are Captain W. A. Fellowes, H.R.H. the Duke of Gloucester and Sir Piers Legh

dipping, and most of them disconcertingly close. It is as if each ball, to revert to cricket, was bowled by a different member of the team. But even in this impossible circumstance you would still know from where the ball was coming, and when. Not so with shooting.

On this occasion the King was master of the situation for the greater part of the drive. He was on the right of the line and had to contend as well with a great many partridges which swung up to him, almost taking his cap off, to continue up the hedge. Partridges retreating on the swing at a fine angle, slightly above head height but dropping, can be very awkward birds, and the King's display of varied skill was a joy to perceive.

Towards the end of the drive he struck a bad patch. It is not easy to assume a rhythm of action, as you may in cricket, when every bird is different from the last. It is often the sudden appearance of a slow, ponderous bird which momentarily unbalances you. Your action is fast, but the bird is slow. You are out of gear. So on this occasion the King suddenly blazed off two barrels at a single partridge idling over the stubble, and the charge on each occasion sent up a spurt of dust some feet in front of the bird. Had there been a pause then all might have been well, but the skirmish continued with the uninterrupted sound of keepers' whistles and coveys whirring about the line. For a few moments the King could not regain his composure, and a succession of double misses ensued to the verbal accompaniment of self-depreciation. And then all at once he was in balance again, and was wreathed in smiles as he became once more the steady expert.

October 9th, 1947　WEST ACRE　*Abbey Farm*
　24　pheasants　　H. Birkbeck, H. Birkbeck, junr., C. Birkbeck, O. Birk-
370　partridges　　beck, Coke, W. Fellowes and myself
　1　various
————　　　　　　Fine after early fog. A good lot of partridges.
395
————

Like any other game, good shooting is largely a question of nerves. Many excitable people might possibly shoot better after a strong dose of a sedative, and some have even been known to claim that they have shot 'better than ever' after a 'night out'. Maybe their senses were duller than usual that morning and they did not suffer from jitters and lose their heads. The cure for a bad patch is often to be found in a deep breath, a brief pause, and a fresh start facing the right direction with the correct foot forward. This the King did in due course. But the less composed amongst us often continue for the rest of the day worrying about our continued poor execution. 'One who vexes himself about missing a fair shot is the less likely to support himself at all times as a first-rate performer, because that vexation alone might be the very means of his missing other shots, and therefore he could not be so much depended on as another man who bore the disappointment with good humour.' The redoubtable Hawker bequeathed this hint to the shooting community over one hundred years ago —yet to-day we hear every factor indicted, from guns, shoulders, backs, bruised fingers, the light, food, drink and a host of more original items. More plausible explanations might be the Kremlin, a temperamental cook, school fees, and so on—in fact, anything that causes distraction and a reduction in complete attention. That is why a generous and considerate host, who is so anxious to see his guests enjoy a well-devised and executed day, sometimes has the misfortune to be off his best form, for his own performance has not a call on his undivided attention.

In one other vital respect the King was an object-lesson to all

---

November 14th, 1947   St. Paul's Walden   *Hitch Wood* and *Easthall*

549	pheasants	David L., Michael L., Salisbury, J. Morrison,
10	partridges	P. Fleming, Joey L. and myself
4	rabbits	
4	various	Fine but dull. A very nice day. Birds flew well.

567

who handle a gun. He always turned towards his bird, and his footwork was faultless. *Feet*—how often this pre-eminent factor in shooting is ignored! It is a strange thing that feet are considered of incalculable importance in every game, yet often totally ignored in this one pursuit. In golf, feet, we are told, are a major consideration (the target being stationary at your feet). In cricket again, feet are a fundamental in the successful technique of batting (the target is visible in the bowler's hand and all the way to the bat, and apart from swing or break according to the prowess of the bowler, it cannot suddenly change its mind and alter direction). And yet again, feet are vital in tennis because they determine balance, and without balance you cannot serve or drive or volley effectively (and here the ball is white, and always visible from the source of approach, having no self-determination in flight after its propulsion by your opponent).

Yet with a bird, which may appear from any quarter, even from behind, and which can alter course at will, which can accelerate or pull up, which can climb or dive—and finally, which is a living, whirring creature in whose immediate presence even the most accomplished sometimes experience a blurring of their faculties and just blaze off—with this unpredictable target, feet are perhaps the last lesson which is mentioned to the young sportsman. In the early years of boyhood-shooting safety, which must come first, and many other lessons are taught; but very rarely the matter of footwork and the need to turn towards the bird. In this respect the nimble action of the King, his lightness on his feet and his readiness to move instantaneously, constituted a prime contribution to his frequent brilliance.

It is often after the second movement of the proceedings on any shoot that one enjoys a sense of elation or is burdened with mounting disappointment. On a partridge beat one has usually seen enough at this stage to know either that there are plenty of birds, or that there are fewer than expected; and on this occasion it was clear that there were enough for a bag which should satisfy the most demanding—for all in this party there were ample to afford a fine day's sport. The coveys were large and strong, there had been no blank spells, and the bulk of the birds had moved in the right direction, on to ground which was now to be driven. The beaters moved on without pause, the little piles of game were collected and taken down to the old covered wagon and hung in rows by the picturesque character who had charge of it (a notable character indeed, in a great overcoat given him by a former Earl of Leicester, which he wears firmly buttoned up to the neck in summer or winter, sun or snow), and the King mounted his Land-rover and was carried, to save his leg, across the stubbles and through the lanes to the next stand.

The following drive was a successful one. A wide sweep of country was flanked into a beet field which the guns now headed, and through praiseworthy co-ordination and timing the party was able to watch the coveys gliding swiftly into it from three directions. This is always an encouraging feature and provokes high anticipation. The thick cover ahead seemed now to be packed with birds, and the party waited in silent suspense as the bobbing figures of the beaters appeared over a wide horizon and converged to re-form in a half-moon round the far side of the beet.

The hedge was low, but intermittent trees stretched the length of the line, and the guns stood back. The partridges, coming downwind, broke through the trees from all quarters; they would head for a gap, and then, seeing a gun, swerve through another. Thus for the guns they were constantly sweeping unsuspected from behind a tree at a great pace, and were a fine test of skill and action. There were a great many pheasants as well, which sailed for the line among the partridges, and called for that extra ounce of concentration as one switched from one species to another. The King scored a beautiful right and left out of a high covey, and then changing guns quickly seemed certain to repeat the performance on a pheasant and a single partridge wheeling towards him. But then he missed the pheasant with the first shot, though he killed the partridge cleanly with the second. As well he scored three convincing mixed doubles at pheasants and partridges, and at the end of the drive had a bag of 30 head to retrieve.

The true sportsman is always away to pick up his birds as soon as the beaters have tapped out the final hedge in front, and this characteristic was most noticeable in the King. He usually worked his own dog himself, and, when a guest, his head keeper, Edward Dodd, also stood by him with a couple of the excellent Sandringham dogs in hand. Dodd made straight for the distant birds or for a runner, whilst the King collected up the rest of the bag into a pile by his stand. This was a business-like procedure, and not at all the casual interlude that it is for some, who are content to tell others roughly where their birds are, and then to relax in idle chatter as they wander on. The King had not finished his shoot, and was not ready for conversation, until the birds were found. Picking up was an inseparable part of the shoot itself—the game began when he occupied his stand and finished when the last bird was recovered.

It should not be assumed that this practice was just one more piece of evidence of His Majesty's unfailing thoroughness. The King's conduct after a drive was, in fact, an example of the manner in which *every man who handles a gun* should proceed at the end of a drive. Absolute thoroughness at the pick-up is, in fact, nothing more than common humanity, and casualness is nothing less than absolute cruelty. Shooting should not be cruel, but as practised by many to-day it is. In two respects many sportsmen weaken the case of the shooting community as a whole, first by firing long shots and thus risking the wounding of birds which travel too far to be marked and retrieved (how often one hears a man remark, *with satisfaction*, 'I hit that bird!'), and secondly, through idleness or some similar shortcoming, by not persevering, whatever the climatic conditions or the thickness of the covert,

---

October 8th, 1947 HOLKHAM *Burnham Thorpe*
26 pheasants Leicester, Coke, Templewood, Hardwicke, S. Van
404 partridges Neck, C. McLean, W. Fellowes and myself
6 hares
1 rabbit
—— Fine. W. wind. Saw a nice lot of birds.
437

until they are confident that no wounded creature is left to suffer. If the programme for the rest of the party is likely to be affected by delay, then a man with a dog or the sportsman himself should be left behind until the job has been completed. In all these respects the King was most emphatic.

The impartial Report of the Committee on Cruelty to Wild Animals (1951) stated, in regard to shooting: 'The shooting of wild animals of all kinds is very widely practised both as a method of control and for sport. If the animal fired at were always killed outright, shooting would be one of the most humane methods of control, but this is by no means always the case and there can be no doubt that it may involve great suffering if the animal is wounded and escapes, particularly if it is not followed up and killed. This happens less frequently with experienced shots, but we think a great deal of shooting is done by people who lack the necessary skill and experience.' These are fair words, and offenders might well take to heart the good example set by the King.

At Holkham the day had now brightened and the wind was stronger. For the next movement it would blow directly down the line, across the flight of the birds. No. 1 gun was in the right-hand corner of the hedge, but No. 7 was fully a hundred yards from his corner and with the wind blowing strongly from 1 to 7, surely many birds would be blown towards 7, and even pass outside the line in the wide gap where there was no gun? So it appeared to the King, and he said as much to a young companion as they walked across the field towards the line. The King was No. 5 and, with the wind as it was, might he not be 'out of it', and the bulk of birds even miss the line altogether? Had the host considered this point, or observed what influence the freshening wind might have? Might it be sensible to call his attention to it, lest a good drive, where the coveys were now calling excitedly, should be spoilt? Thus the conversation went and the companion said, 'Shall I mention it to him, Sir?' With royal assent he marched purposefully off to find his host. The host looked doubtful, and asked, 'What does the King think?' 'He agrees.' In the end the line moved. No. 1 was left blank, everyone moved down one, and

No. 7 went in the left-hand space. This felt much better, the wind was blowing strongly towards the left, and the last three guns could already imagine the coveys swerving with the wind towards them.

The drive began and very soon the partridges, which had been packed into a confined space and were now apprehensive and very much on the alert, began to jump up, one covey following another without interruption, and pass in a steady stream over the line. But consternation reigned on the left of the line, for the three guns there were listening to a merry barrage on the right, but had no participation in it. The partridges veered straight back into the wind and returned to the ground from which they had been moved. No. 7 was out of it, No. 6 had the odd shot, and the King killed four or five single birds. Nos. 1 to 4 had an excellent shoot. The King watched his neighbour No. 4 thoroughly enjoying himself just inside the partridge front, at the peg where he should have been himself.

Of course it is an elementary lesson. The man on the spot knows, the visitor does not. 'They always go that way,' said a member of the host's family, 'and not even a hurricane will divert them.'

This was the sort of situation that the King really enjoyed. The young guest had stuck his neck out, and the axe was waiting for him. It was, of course, he, not the King, who had insisted on moving the line. 'We are all very glad to know that you have some ideas,' said His Majesty, 'but have you any better ideas?'

October 10th, 1947 MASSINGHAM *The Heath*
127 pheasants O. Birkbeck, Coke, H. Cator, L. Londsdale, C. McLean,
259 partridges W. Fellowes and myself
 12 hares
  7 rabbits Fine. W. wind. A v. nice day and birds flew very well.
  1 woodcock
  3 various

409

The last suggestion had betrayed a lack of intuition, of fieldcraft, and perhaps he should gain further experience before meddling with the Holkham drill which had been found quite acceptable for some generations.

There was to be no remorse, and at a later stand the King was after him again. 'What are your suggestions for this drive? We hope you have some ideas.' And further on, 'Where would you like us to stand here? Should we cross the hedge and face in the opposite direction?' It became a standard jest, and months later, on a bleak January day on the Broads when a party was about to occupy sturdy reed and timber butts out in the water, the King called from one punt to another, 'Shouldn't you move these butts before the drive, with the wind where it is?'

There were two more drives before luncheon, the first a novel and exciting experience where the partridges are driven over a farmhouse and its buildings. Here, without sharp alertness, successful performance is impossible. When birds approach from behind any form of vegetation some small degree of warning is often received, be it only the sound of wings or a glimpse of movement through the uppermost branches of the hedge. But over the tiled roofs of big barns they seem to be suddenly catapulted into space over your head from nowhere, as clay-pigeons from a trap. And one is inclined to wait perhaps a fraction longer than usual, being hesitant to fire too near a roof, whereas one has no disinclination to pepper a hedge. Thus the partridges, coming downhill as well, are often over you before you kill your first bird, and this is one place where a great many are taken behind.

And this was the one stand where the King was definitely out of it. Standing on the left of the line he killed but three birds. For no apparent cause the majority missed his corner altogether. The host can control the beaters or the guns, but outside certain limits he cannot control the birds. This host, slightly discomfited, on hearing someone from the other end of the line say he had killed 18 partridges, asked him in an undertone to keep quiet about it. But such events cannot be concealed from the most observant man in the kingdom. He knew all right.

But the King understood these matters as well as anyone, and whilst indulging in a little of his accustomed ragging, his enjoyment of this excellent day was fully sustained.

After the next drive the Daimler brake carried the party to the little Burnham Thorpe manor, which with the ancient church stands in secluded serenity beyond the northern boundary of the village. The stream winds round it, and snipe rise from its marshy fringe by the entrance gate. Teal rest on a little pool less than a stone's throw from the house, and all about the partridges call in the stubble fields or cluster along the farm roads in search of dust and grit. This was the luncheon setting, in the home of the host's sister, Silvia Combe, with the autumn sunlight playing a silver melody on the old flint walls and the ancient willows dancing a sparkling rhythm against a lively sky.

Well within the hour the party emerged, and social gossip is better confined to the observation that all were in high spirits, and indeed why not after an exhilarating morning of 300 head and a merry luncheon to follow? Six guns entered the bus, but a relative of the host was missing. Eventually he appeared in some confusion, protesting many apologies, to say that his cap was nowhere to be found. But at once he spotted it upon the head of another member already seated in the bus, so it was then his cap that had to be found. In due course all these vital pieces of equipment were located, and distributed correctly, and then the brake proceeded down the sandy lane towards the world of tarmac once more.

November 14th, 1950 ST. PAUL'S WALDEN *Reynolds Wood*

317	pheasants	David Lyon, Dalhousie, I. Walker, J. Harrison, W.
24	partridges	Hill-Wood, Joey L. and myself
11	hares	
6	rabbits	
3 (1)	woodcock	Fine. W. wind. As always a perfect day.
2	pigeons	
12	various	

375

The destination was the true centre of the proceedings, the
pivot of the Burnham shoot. Just as every good argument has a
point, or as every artistic composition should have a basic
feature to which all others are related, so a good shoot is con-
ceived to afford the optimum display at the most advantageous
point. On some shoots there may be a main feature in the morning
and another in the afternoon. This is true at Burnham, but in a
sense the morning and afternoon features are one and the same,
since the guns stand in the same place but merely turn about.

The main stand of the morning was, in fact, the last drive before
luncheon, to which all previous drives were planned to make a
contribution. A short interval then occurs—and it has to be a
brief one, or partridges will start to move back to their own
ground voluntarily—and immediately afterwards the guns take
post in the same valley for the return drive off the western slopes.
Thus this valley, with a rivulet trickling through its narrow
meadow, is the true hinge of the day.

There are many humble plots of earth in this land which in
themselves possess no marked distinction by contrast with any
other plots, but for the sporting activity which they have supported for decades they are justly famous. By geographical location, and by the shape of the ground, a mere field, or a wood, or a
point on a marsh, may earn a reputation of renown in sporting
history. Thus Cockshoot Broad will live on unchallenged;
Scarborough Clump at Holkham is synonymous with high
pheasants; a wood called Signal Hill near Cambridge possesses
probably an unassailable record for pigeons, and certainly no
other strip of meadow, such as that unostentatious feature in the
Burnham Thorpe valley, can possess such a rich and glorious
history in the annals of partridge driving. Across its narrow span,
over two thick hedges with many trees, hundreds of thousands of
partridges have swept in lofty and rapid flight. On its turf the
paragons of shooting have felt their barrels grow hot, and impressive bags for single drives have been recorded from time to
time.

In 1924 eighty brace were picked up for the return drive. A

veteran keeper was describing the event to the right-hand gun on the day which is the subject of this chapter. There was a wonderful stock of partridges, according to his account, and the luncheon interval was a trifle late after the intense activity of the morning. The interval itself was a shade longer than usual, since the spectacular proceedings of the morning were probably conducive to prolonged discussion. Meanwhile a great many partridges started to move back of their own accord across the valley, so that when the guns occupied their stands the drive had, so to speak, already begun. Shooting from the outset was consistent and intense. A great many birds broke through a gap in the trees on the right of the line, over the right shoulder of No. 1 gun. This was described vividly by the keeper because his listener, No. 1 on this occasion, was now occupying the exact spot. 'The trouble was,' said the old man, with earnest solemnity, and no flicker of frivolity, 'that the Captain couldn't hit no birds on his roight at all—you see, that was after lunch.'

The audience was left wondering if he had attached the correct significance to this observation, since it was made without humour as if the second part, quite naturally and logically, followed the first. His *malaise* was enhanced when a covey took him completely by surprise and swept through the selfsame gap, to the right flank, and was missed with both barrels. The temptation to protest that this was not due to luncheon was resisted as being unlikely, in the circumstances, to sound convincing.

November 15th, 1950 St. Paul's Walden *Hitch Wood* and *Easthall*

346	pheasants	David Lyon, I. Walker, Dunglass, J. Morrison, Tryon
4	partridges	and myself
2	hares	
3	rabbits	Damp and showery. Did very well considering the con-
1	woodcock	ditions.
1	pigeon	
7	various	

364

Both these operations in the valley, from east to west, are what we have already described as 'good stands'. The partridges fly well, some wheel along the line, and many spectacular kills are secured high in the air. The King on this day, confronted with a profusion of inspiring targets, was at the height of his form, and killed cleanly 18 birds over the first hedge, and 22 on the return, as well as a number of pheasants.

And here was revealed one small fragment of evidence of the thought which the host had given to his planning of this delightful day. In the ultimate field of the main stand, the first drive over the valley, there was a narrow strip of kale running down the field, at right angles to the line of guns. It was no more than twenty yards wide, but it was the only cover in a bare field. Any partridges which settled short of the line would certainly pitch in it, and all the pheasants would be there. And the strip of roots finished exactly opposite the King. Thus it became apparent why he had started the day as No. 6. The mathematical contortion of calculating six drives backwards, moving down two each time, might tax the resources of many a rugged sportsman, but not the Earl of Leicester.

There were two more drives that afternoon, on the slopes to the west of the village, and the quality of manoeuvre and the sufficiency of game was maintained to the last. The wind had now subsided, and a glorious autumn afternoon was in being. High clouds suffused with the most delicate wash of pink and orange were poised motionless against a sky that was neither blue, nor green, nor grey, but a restrained hue of its own which combined all three. The stubbles took on a russet glow, and the long but

---

October 17th, 1950 HOLKHAM *Burnham Thorpe*
74 pheasants Leicester, R. Coke, C. Dunbar, A. Buxton, M. Adeane,
440 partridges Joey L. and myself
9 hares
___ Fine. Saw a nice lot of birds.
523

gentle shadows of autumn afternoon had a warmer tone. Partridges, after a day of disturbance, were now calling to each other all about and re-forming once more on their own territories, and curlews sailed overhead towards the saltings with melodious calls that were sharp and clear in the stillness.

The company made its way, after the last pick-up, across the fields towards the village—guns, keepers, loaders, beaters and dogs. The Daimler and the old game wagon were there, and a rough estimate of the bag was being hastily prepared. On a grass verge, silent and smiling, the inhabitants of this Norfolk hamlet were waiting to see the King. Eventually this diverse company was gathered about the car, with His Majesty in the centre shaking hands in farewell to each friend and keeper in turn—a group which was a cross-section of the Norfolk community he knew and loved so well, farmers, farmworkers, their wives and children, keepers, his neighbours and friends. The King, with a last glance towards everyone, stepped aboard. And as the purring motor pulled away silently along the rustic lane, a little forest of hats, caps, hands and handkerchiefs was held aloft.

VIII

BROADLAND ADVENTURES

We have seen earlier how the King's interest in duck-shooting developed rapidly after the first opportunities he had of flighting, and how this interest took effect momentously once he was in a position to put Sandringham to practical purpose in this respect. During the years which followed, his experience was broadened by regular visits to duck shoots other than at Sandringham.

The most attractive feature of wildfowling is the variety which it offers. This is afforded in the first place by geographical location. On marshes and flooded meadows near the sea, or on daytime resting-places such as the Broads, mallard, wigeon and teal may be, as a rule, the main element in the bag; but if the weather is appropriate, the balance may often be tipped in favour of diving ducks. On inland ponds and splashes mallard and teal are again the most likely arrivals, but in all these separate areas there is always the chance of many other species, shoveler, golden-eye, pintail and so on.

To give the sport yet greater diversity, the same species may behave differently in different places. Further, the same species may behave differently in the same place in different weather. Thus duck-shooting can never be monotonous; of all sports with the shotgun none is more generous in its bestowal of uncertainty, surprise, disappointment, excitement, astonishment, and other desirable or less welcome features.

The Norfolk Broads is one area where almost every form of duck-shooting is available. The locality presents a very different picture in winter to that so familiar to the public from personal observation on summer holidays, or from railway posters. The blue sunlit waters which mirror white sails and chromium-fitted launches in the warm weather become cold and forbidding in winter, a choppy grey under a leaden sky or a chill paleness in frost and fog. The green of reed-beds changes to russet and chrome, and the marshland trees, recently dense clumps of foliage in a jungle of bramble and sedge, assume a witch-like character as they point bare and crooked fingers as the wind bids them. There is total desolation, no sail nor launch disturbs the abandoned scene. Perhaps a lone Spartan pike-fishing from an anchored punt presents the only human movement in a desolate scene.

This setting, for the naturalist or duck shooter, is sheer enchantment. For the rest it is, perhaps mercifully, most unattractive. But the Broads can accommodate all tastes in the appropriate season, and the important areas are now safely in the care of the Norfolk Naturalists Trust, and thus scientific assets and the public interest are alike protected for all time.

For the duck shooter, however, in His Majesty's day, there were teal and mallard on evening flight by ponds and splashes, and again in the morning on their resting-places; wigeon and diving ducks on the open water in the morning or during a rough day, separate places in gale and storm, other chances in snow and ice. It was no impossibility to secure perhaps ten different species of duck in a single bag, not to mention snipe, golden plover, coots, hooded-crows and other eccentrics which passed the butt. This unique land was a wildfowler's paradise, where a feast of varied and exhilarating experiences could be enjoyed in a matter of hours.

It is not surprising that the King, as a neighbour in the county, became a Broadland figure of repute. And such was his enthusiasm that he often came there, not just for one shoot, but for serious flighting expeditions. Like any good wildfowler he fixed his visits by the weather, and the records of these interludes are among the most fascinating in all the prolific pages of the game book. One such spell was in the winter of 1938.

The outlook at the New Year promised well for wildfowling. A frost gripped the countryside so that ditches and ponds,

splashes and swamps were icebound and still. The duck were ex-
cluded from their accustomed haunts dispersed about the county,
and were concentrated along the coastline and on the few inland
reserves where the abundance of fowl prevented a freeze-up, or on
feeding-grounds where the water was kept open for them. A
sudden blizzard reversed the pattern of the scene, so that instead
of a dark landscape under a lighter sky, a leaden greyness above
defined with unreal clarity the silent whiteness of the horizon. In
the fields the huddled forms of partridges looked like black sods
of earth, and the gulls which drifted in from the saltings were like
aimless snowflakes at the mercy of a squall. Packed squads of
waders wheeled with baffling unison over the mudflats, and beyond duck in great numbers rode the turgid waves, looking from
the shore like black pencil lines across the seascape. Inland, in
contrast to the bare lifelessness of the fields, the few remaining
reaches of open water in broadland were scenes of congested
activity. The silence was broken by the whistling of teal and
wigeon and the raucous quacking of mallard.

The King, as was the Christmas custom, was at Sandringham.
Now was the moment to go after duck, and so the plans for
covert shooting were promptly abandoned and the royal car
headed eastwards in a swirl of powdered snow. As the party
reached Woodbastwick[1] the weather was worsening, and in a

1 Woodbastwick Hall, near Ranworth Broad, the home of Colonel Cator.

January 3rd, 1938	WOODBASTWICK *Ranworth Flood*
43 mallard	Harry Cator, Joey Legh, Michael Lyon, Colin McLean,
4 wigeon	Percy Perrin and myself
1 shoveler	
3 teal	Fine. Very calm. Evening flight.
29 tufted duck	
21 pochard	
1 scaup	
3 snipe	

105

WINDSOR
*The King plucks the pin feather from
the wing of a woodcock*

HICKLING
The end of a sunny day

few hours a heavy snowfall had obliterated the minor undulations of the ground. But the preliminary operation was now complete—the King was in the area, in the right weather, with three days in hand for the use of every opportunity which might present itself. This was to be not a duck shoot, but a flighting session. And everything seemed absolutely right; the assembled friends were full of hope. But, as so often happens, the sport of duck-shooting, despite all its fascination, was to cheat its loyalists once more. This time conditions were to prove too good.

The King and his companions arrived at Woodbastwick for luncheon on January 2nd and a three-day plan was evolved in eager consultation. Outside the wintry scene proclaimed with grim assurance that a cold spell had come to stay. However, intermittent snow showers made the party hopeful that the weather would remain rough without too much frost, and at all costs it was hoped that the open Broads would not become frozen over. Soon the car was out once more on the deserted by-roads on the way to Hickling. The maroon Daimler, speckled with frozen snowflakes, moved silently over the last stretch of the snow-carpeted drive to the shooting lodge.

In summer, sedge- and reed-warblers chatter a staccato chorus in the dykes alongside, grasshopper warblers reel in the thick marsh grass, and harriers beat lazily about their territories on either side. The strange booming of the bittern, the 'bitterbum or bogbumper' of an earlier age, punctuates the stillness like a phantom double bass.

But to-day it was a harsh spectacle, the dykes lifeless and solid with ice, reeds and long grass frosted and fast. No birds spoke in the bleak afternoon on the marshland, and only the duck shooters' accustomed abundance of optimism would have explained to the unversed the merry countenances of the company which fore-gathered for tea at the lodge.

This white, reed-thatched bungalow stands on an island lawn amongst the reed-beds, surrounded by dykes and channels which lead out to the open water and to the Broad proper. The ice was thick and snow-covered in the channels, and in the normal event

the lodge would have been sealed off altogether and no movement
from it afloat would have been possible. However, Jim Vincent,
the head keeper, and his men, in expectation of a visit by His
Majesty, had worked continuously and hard in their punts and
succeeded in keeping a passage-way clear of ice so that it was
possible to reach Swimcotes Slad[1] on the opposite side of the
Broad. Here again a small expanse of water had been kept clear
each day for the duck at evening flight. During the night the birds,
by constant swimming and dibbling, and by the warmth of their
bodies, keep the water open themselves. But each afternoon the
keepers must smash up the newly formed skin and scoop the
broken ice out of the water. This is essential, since once the last
few inches of water disappear the duck will cease to come. It is not
necessary, however, to keep open more than a diminutive pond.
The duck do not have to swim, and they do not require water on
which to settle. In such conditions they usually land on the ice.
But they do need a drink after a meal, and great numbers of duck
can drink during the night from a tiny pool. Without the drink,
however, they will go elsewhere for food.

Vincent quanted[2] the King through the passage, breaking as
they progressed a thin skin of ice which was already forming
again on the surface. As they neared Swimcotes, a stream of coots
flew back over the punt and the King had a merry *battue* from his
seat, killing thirty, which mostly fell on the ice and were retrieved

[1] Slad is a Broadland term for a shallow stretch of water on the marshes.
[2] The Broadland term for the local method of punting.

January 2nd, 1939   HICKLING BROAD
30 mallard   H. Cator, Michael Lyon, Joey L., Colin McLean,
 2 shoveler   P. Perrin and myself
 1 teal
23 tufted duck   N.W. breeze. Ice on the broad and snow. A good even-
24 pochard   ing flight.
 1 golden-eye
33 coots

114

later by the dogs. His Majesty occupied a dry sheltered tub by the side of the slad, and settled in to wait for the flight.

The remainder of the party went to two other slads on the edge of the Broad which could be reached by walking along the banks. As they waited in their tubs the 'old hands' were visited by many misgivings. In spite of the snow and the wind, the frost was as hard as ever. The open Broad was probably steadily freezing over, and after another night of frost it would certainly be completely so. If Hickling was frozen, so would be Ranworth. There was every sign that the hard weather would persist, and it seemed almost certain now that there would be no morning flights. After the high expectation of the forenoon, it looked as if the King's activities might be restricted after all to evening flights by ponds of broken ice.

That evening they enjoyed a sporting flight. But the sky was dark and a light snow fell spasmodically. The duck came early, which was as well since because of the heavy cloud and early darkness it was not long before they were all picking up. The King shot over forty tufted duck and pochard, an exhilarating experience while it lasted. He got as well a handful of mallard and one golden-eye. On the marshland slads there were few divers and the bag was predominantly mallard. The total pick-up was 30 mallard, 2 shoveler, 1 teal, 23 tufted, 24 pochard, 1 golden-eye and 33 coots, a total of 114 head. It was very dark when the King left Swimcotes with Vincent, and falling snow reduced visibility to nil. To be out in the total exposure of East Norfolk within two miles of the North Sea on such a night would not be to everyone's

January 3rd, 1939 WOODBASTWICK *Ranworth Flood*

109	mallard	H. Cator, Michael Lyon, Joey L., Colin McLean, P.
1	teal	Perrin and myself
15	tufted duck	
9	pochard	Evening flight. Fine and still. Duck came in very well to
9	coots	us from 3.0–5.0 p.m. Good fun. I got 47.

143

taste, but for the King, his punt carrying a cargo of plump diving ducks, it was enthralling.

Back at Woodbastwick that evening it was recognised that without a sudden break in the weather and an overnight thaw the morning flight planned on Ranworth and Cockshoot Broads was off. After dinner the frost still had a firm grip and the last hope was abandoned. The next day was not passed in housebound idleness, however, and a sporting expedition was improvised with four keepers as beaters. A wintry skirmish in the frosted coverts yielded 45 pheasants, 2 woodcock, 7 pigeons and a jay.

The party was back early in the afternoon to put on waders and extra clothing for an evening flight. After being denied the duck for nearly twenty-four hours, all were impatient to be on a marsh again, and in good time they went to the Flood, an area of shallow swamp to the east of Ranworth Broad, where on this occasion quite a large stretch of water had been kept open by the keepers. By ill fortune the weather was now fine and still, though very cold, but even without a wind they picked up 109 mallard, 1 teal, 15 tufted, 9 pochard and 9 coots. The King notes in his game book, 'duck came in very well to us from 3 to 5 p.m. Good fun. I got 47'. This was an excellent evening's bag, and in spite of the disappointment caused by the frozen broads in the morning, His Majesty was delighted with the outcome.

And the flight seems to have whetted everyone's appetite for more, for all were determined to devise some form of operation for next morning despite the freeze-up. At Hickling the lodge stands opposite a narrow-way of water which joins up the big broad to a much smaller broad to the eastward known as The Sounds. In normal conditions, and particularly in rough weather, diving ducks often fly from one end to the other during the daytime, and it is possible to have some enjoyable but spasmodic shooting from butts in the narrow-way within 100 yards of the lodge. It was thought that even in ice conditions there might be some movement going on, and since this was the only possible proposition which could be thought of, it was agreed that the party should assemble again at Hickling next morning.

Snow fell heavily during the night, and Colin McLean had a rough trip next day from Dereham. Nevertheless he and Percy and Meredith Perrin were assembled at the lodge at nine o'clock. They waited for some time with no news of the King, until finally at ten-thirty a message was brought by a policeman to say that the royal car had been snowed up on the way, and had been forced to turn back. There was no longer any object in their waiting, and although there was now a blizzard and the wind cut the skin, the three of them took up positions in the adjacent butts. They were in luck, for the diving duck, frozen out of their accustomed haunts, were restless and constantly on the move, and they had some real rough weather wildfowling in classical if most inhospitable conditions. They survived the rigours until nearly two o'clock, and collected 7 mallard, 1 teal, 28 tufted, 18 pochard, 2 scaup, 3 golden-eye, 1 hybrid tufted-pochard and 14 coots. Colin, after a hazardous return journey, was fortunate to reach base.

This was the end of the King's Broadland visit on that occasion. After the high expectations with which he set forth, it must have been something of a disappointment that the schedule was in the end cut to only two evening flights.

But no doubts remain about the degree of his love for marshland shooting, and reflecting on this event, it is an inspiring thought for sportsmen that the King was snowed up in a blizzard trying to get through to what was, at the best, only the off-chance of some duck—in conditions which must have seemed, before he set out on a ten-mile journey, almost impossible for motor travel.

· · · · · ·

January 17th, 1939 RANWORTH *The Broad* and *Cockshoot*

168	wild duck	Harry Cator, Joey Legh, Colin McLean, Oliver Birkbeck,
21	shoveler	Percy Perrin and myself
42	teal	
1	pigeon	Morning flight. Fine and calm. In butts from 6.0 a.m. to
——		12.0 noon. I got 68 on Cockshoot.
232		
——		

Wildfowling, like salmon fishing, favours the man who lives on the spot. It is very unusual in either case for the distant worker to strike the right moment frequently, either at weekends or during holidays. And even the man who is ready to leave his office promptly in response to a trunk call will often travel for several hours all agog with anticipation, to find on his arrival that weather or water conditions have already changed for the worse. This disadvantage, as we have seen, was the lot of the King as much as of anyone else.

The winter of 1937–8 was quite exceptional for the number of duck that were in Norfolk, and there was one occasion during that season when everything went right for the King.

It may happen only once in a shooting lifetime that a man can reflect on a wildfowling occasion and say 'from first to last every hope was fulfilled to perfection'. After the best of red-letter events there is nearly always at least one aspect, if not more, which could have been slightly better. It is not that duck shooters are hard to please—the reverse is the truth—but there are so many varied factors which influence a duck shoot that the odds are weighed heavily against them all being favourable at any one moment. First, the ideal occasion demands a plentiful attendance of duck themselves. This in itself is conditioned by a host of contributory factors. Secondly, the weather should be right for the particular locality. Thirdly, a good wind. Fourth, the wind in the right direction. Fifth, a good shooting light, and the party's arrival in position at the right moment. Further, one likes to shoot well, to have a good pick-up; and lastly, to feel, after it is all over, that one has not overdone things and that the duck will soon

---

January 2nd, 1946   WOODBASTWICK   *Ranworth Flood*
   2   rabbits   H. Cator, Michael Lyon, Joey L. and myself
   3 (2) woodcock
 101   mallard   Evening flight. Fine and cold. Duck came in well to all of
   —   us. I got 37.
 106

settle down again after the bombardment and provide good sport on another day. On the occasion now to be reviewed all these requirements were forthcoming in good measure.

At the New Year on Ranworth Broad there was a great gathering of mallard and between three and four hundred wigeon. On Cockshoot Broad to the westward, which is shallow and more swampy, there rested throughout the daylight hours an unprecedented number of teal. Harry Cator had been watching them for several days in fervent hope that they would remain until conditions were right for a shoot.

On January 3rd there was a good west breeze and the King arrived from Sandringham in the afternoon. The evening flight took place on the Flood, and any hope which the party entertained gained further encouragement by the behaviour of the duck that evening. The main feature was the spectacular arrival of numerous parties of diving duck which plummeted out of the sky and had obviously travelled a great distance. They swung round in the wind and came particularly well to the King, who was shooting beautifully right up to the last light. This was a short but concentrated flight, and as one present described it, it was 'fast and furious'. The total bag was 43 mallard, 4 wigeon, 1 shoveler, 3 teal, 29 tufted duck, 21 pochard, 1 scaup, 3 snipe, making a total of 105.

That evening at Woodbastwick every circumstance warmly supported the high anticipation which the company justly felt. They had had a first-class evening flight, which brought glowing contentment. The wind was still blowing encouragingly from the west after dinner, and the great concourse of duck had rested again on the Broads all day, and there was no cause to doubt that they would come back at dawn. The cream of Norfolk duck shooters had never gone to bed in such a state of excitement, and a final flurry took place in the gun-room where some members anxiously counted cartridges once more, in an attempt to convince themselves that they had enough.

The natural sequel to any such wildfowling tale is surely that they went out next morning, groaning under the cartridge load, and never fired a shot. The experienced fenman, on reading of it, would hardly lift an eyebrow. But this is the fairy-tale of wild-fowling stories, and we are not to be let down by such common-place developments. Instead we can read on, breathless, as the perfect duck-shooting tale unfolds.

It is not necessary to record that anyone could not be roused from his bed next morning, or that any member of the party was late for parade. And certainly it would be a safe wager that His Majesty was by no means the last to be astir. He was, for any flight, whatever the prospects, almost invariably the first out of bed in the comfortless chill of the early hours, and often at Sandringham his impatience to be on the move caused him to reach his butt a good hour before the flight began. On the morning of January 4th, 1938, with the wind moaning in the darkness outside, these tendencies were doubtless accentuated, and the company assembled downstairs feeling remarkably alive for that hour of the night.

The allotted positions were occupied in good time before it was light enough to see a duck. The King was taken by his host to Cockshoot, where it was hoped that they would get in amongst the teal, and the four other guns went to the northern flank of Ranworth Broad to deal with the mallard and wigeon. The wind, west with a touch of north, was stronger even than any had dared to hope, as can be judged from the fact that the Ranworth party heard during the morning the tremendous bombardment at Cock-

---

January 3rd, 1946   WOODBASTWICK   *Ranworth Broad*

2	pheasants	H. Cator, Michael Lyon, Joey L., Fergie Lyon, F. Cator
90	mallard	and myself
6	teal	
6	wigeon	Fine and v. cold. Morning flight. There was ice in the
2	pigeons	bays. I got 46.
6	various	

---

shoot, whereas the two there heard hardly a shot from Ranworth half a mile to the eastward.

We cannot do better than follow the tale from the pens of those who took part. Of the Cockshoot flight, Harry Cator writes, 'I remember warning everybody that if the wind was favourable (west or north-west—and, in fact, it was between the two!) we should have a very good shoot and they should take plenty of cartridges. But even this warning was inadequate to prepare the party for what was to come, and one or two guns were in difficulties before the morning was over. We planned to make a break at about 9.30 a.m., since we knew the dogs would be tired after picking up on the Flood the night before, the Flood being a place which is hard on a dog.

'When we reached our butts there was a steady wind—the light was bad for the early part of the flight with a suspicion of "sea rack",[1] and it was evidently one of those days when wildfowl were moving in off the sea knowing that a hard spell was to follow. The first shot was fired at 6.45 a.m., I think by His Majesty, and as the dawn developed one could see that duck were pouring in in exceptional numbers. They continued to do so for the next two hours.

'His Majesty was shooting brilliantly, most of the time at teal. His butt was so placed that teal were coming at him from all

[1] The sea mist which sometimes occurs inland up to a limited distance.

January 20th, 1948 WOODBASTWICK *Ranworth Flood*
54 pheasants   H. Cator, J. Cator, Michael L., Joey L. and myself
10 partridges
1 rabbit   p.m. flight. Still and very cold. Ice on the flood. I had 26
64 mallard   down.
1 teal   (An afternoon drive for pheasants.)
1 pigeon
1 various

angles, and it was a really fine performance. I was near enough to
see how well he was doing and realised that if matters did not ease
up he would soon be wanting more cartridges. At about 9 a.m.
Dick Browne, one of the keepers, arrived after a final pick-up on
the Flood and confirmed that His Majesty was running short, and
so I quanted across with about 100 of my own. The King told me
then that he had about 150 duck down. This was such an exceptional bag that we decided to shoot on for another half-hour
only and then stop to pick-up.

'There was no point in shooting more ducks than we could re-
cover, since the dogs were already tired, and picking up on Cockshoot is almost impossible without dogs, most of the area being
bog and swamp.

'By 9.45 a.m. the King had knocked down 179, of which 173
were picked, and I had killed 89. The picking-up lasted most of
the morning and during that time duck and teal were coming in
the whole time. There is no doubt that, had we elected to stay in
our butts and continue shooting, another 100 duck could have
been shot on Cockshoot alone, not to mention the big broad at
Ranworth.'

Colin McLean went with the remainder of the party to Ranworth Broad, and now describes the fortunes there.

'There were three guns on the north shore of the Broad and
one on a small island about 100 yards from the shore, opposite a
weeded point about halfway from the western end.

'Michael Bowes-Lyon drew No. 1 (the island), Sir Piers Legh
(No. 2) was to start at the island pool in the trees, and Percy
Perrin was No. 4 at the edge of the reeds some seventy yards
to the south of me.

'In the strong north-westerly wind the duck came in over Ranworth marshes and hugged the shelter of the trees along the north
side of the Broad, some making for the little pools in the area
between Sir Piers and myself—and others for the shelter of the big
reed-beds at the western end of the water.

'The hinterland to the north of the Broad is one vast swamp
with a mass of alder, sallow, and a few birch trees, and after hiding

up the boats at the edge of the Broad two of the keepers and their dogs stayed back some distance in the trees, picking up any duck which fell back, and later on, whenever there was a lull in the shooting, searching the reeds and swamp nearer at hand, since with the strong wind and thick undergrowth they were evidently invisible to the duck passing overhead.

'In my butt I had to be careful not to blanket No. 2, and as far as possible to confine my attention to duck which were actually coming in on to my own pool, though I got a lot of shooting at birds coming downwind from the direction of No. 1 and 2 butts, and also at duck which turned in my direction whenever Percy Perrin fired.

'From 7 a.m. until about 8.30 a.m. duck literally poured in—chiefly mallard, though before it was really light there were a lot of wigeon, and the shooting was almost continuous.

'There was a lull for a short time at about 8.30 a.m., giving us the chance of a hot drink and a sandwich, but it was not long before a second flight started. This time there were many more teal and several shoveler, which had probably been diverted from their favourite resting-ground on Cockshoot Broad, from which direction we could hear steady shooting.

'At about 9.30 we received an S.O.S. from the other two guns that their cartridges were running very low, so P.P. and I, who both had a good supply, sent them enough to keep them going until a boat could go back for more.

'The wind if anything increased after daylight and most of the duck shot by M.B.-L. on the island and Sir Piers on the point drifted right down to the east end of the Broad, where another

---

January 21st, 1948   WOODBASTWICK   *Ranworth Broad*
61   mallard   H. Cator, J. Cator, Michael L., Joey L. and myself
 3   teal
12   coots   a.m. flight. Very still, and duck did not come in too well.
──
76
──

keeper with a boat retrieved them from the mass of foam at the edge of the reed-beds.

'We had had orders to be back at Woodbastwick by midday, so that meant that we had to do our picking-up and be off the Broad by about 11 o'clock. Duck were still pouring in as we left. I reckoned that I had 98 duck down myself by then (60 mallard, 21 teal, 8 shoveler, 7 wigeon, 2 pochard). The dogs had had a very hard morning's work.'

When the two parties met once again at the head of the track leading to Cockshoot, the full scope of their success became apparent, and the total bag revealed amidst much acclamation. The King was 'wreathed in smiles'. The final count was 222 mallard, 214 teal, 41 wigeon, 17 shoveler, 4 pochard and 1 tufted, a total of 499 duck, and 1 various.

In his shooting memoirs Colin McLean has written, 'This I think is a record morning flight for this country, beating by a small margin the bag of 487 duck and 7 greylag geese killed by nine guns on the Downpatrick marshes on November 7th, 1924, and that of 493 duck killed by five guns at Laughton (Lincs.) on October 6th, 1913. Of the latter bag no fewer than 398 were teal. I am sure that personally I have never seen a bigger number of duck coming in. Had we been able to hang on for another hour or two it is quite possible that we would have killed another 100 or so on the big broad, as they were still pouring in when we left.'

And Harry Cator concludes, 'We were anxious to get off the

January 4th, 1938	WOODBASTWICK *Cockshoot* and *Ranworth Broads*
222 mallard	Harry Cator, Joey Legh, Michael Lyon, Colin McLean,
41 wigeon	Percy Perrin and myself
17 shoveler	Morning flight. Showery. N.W. wind. Harry and I
214 teal	were at Cockshoot. I had 173 down. H.C. 89. Duck
1 tufted duck	came in from 7.0 a.m. till 11 a.m. in vast quantities.
4 pochard	
1 various	

500

Broad by midday in order to let the duck in, and to avoid, by not shooting too many, the necessity of disturbing them again by picking-up next day. Had we chosen to stay on and shoot all day, I am sure 800 duck or more could have been shot.'

But to prolong the proceedings after such a magnificent flight, simply for the sake of a big record, would have been entirely out of character with this particular party, and the most agreeable note on which to end is provided by Colin McLean—'Duck were still pouring in when we left,' which is a tribute to the good judgment of the party.

Harry Cator has now established Cockshoot and Ranworth Broads as sanctuaries for all time, and they are not even disturbed by onlookers. Duck and other marshland birds breed there in the spring and summer, and in winter wildfowl of many species congregate there as of old. The whole area is a fitting memorial to the great events of the past, and to the royal wildfowler who took part in them.

After luncheon this superb day was rounded off by a happy interlude in the coverts which yielded 148 wild pheasants, 1 partridge, 1 woodcock, 1 pigeon, 1 hare, 2 rabbits and 1 various, bringing the whole day's total to 655 head, which included thirteen different items.

IX

UNUSUAL OCCASIONS

The fact that large totals have not been permitted to dominate these pages is because in themselves they fail to convey any particular impression, and had the accent been on such events the reader might well have gathered an entirely wrong impression of the King. He was a sportsman of unusual brilliance yet simple tastes, and this could not be deduced from a list of heavy bags.

The fact is that it is not the size of the bag but the quality of the sport which determines whether a day is good or bad. Thirty head may be 'good' on one occasion, and 500 pheasants 'bad' on another, and that the King's standards were not governed by numerical considerations is clearly emphasised in his own notes. After a day when 165 pheasants were killed he remarked, 'A good day, with strong west wind. Birds were wild and difficult,' whilst after a much larger result his only comment was, 'Birds did not fly well.' After a pre-war day of the old style in Wiltshire, he noted, 'A fair day. Birds flew well in places,' whilst a Sandringham shoot late in the season which yielded only 60 head was classified as 'a good sporting day'. The happy family character of the King's shooting is suggested by another Sandringham comment, after only 43 pheasants had been picked-up, 'A very good afternoon. The ladies acted as beaters.'

Perhaps the most acceptable definition of a good day is an occasion which lives up to or exceeds one's expectations. Anticipation plays a dominant rôle in sport and most particularly in shooting, and a great deal of the fun lies in the contemplation of the entertainment ahead. This somehow sheds a warmer glow on the evening beforehand, and one experiences a richer sensation when staying in a house for a day's sport than when paying a visit simply for a night's rest, however indiscreet it might be to admit the fact to one's hostess.

Thus the verdict on a day's shooting is closely allied to one's expectations. But while every sportsman is alive to the possibility of failure, and accepts setbacks cheerfully when they are caused by such natural agencies as the weather or the behaviour of the birds themselves, they are less acceptable when they are the outcome of misleading advice. No true wildfowler is demoralised because ducks fail to flight, but any sportsman may be soundly bored by a bad pheasant shoot. It is not a poor day because one has been defeated by the quarry or thwarted by the elements—these are the welcome hazards of the game. But it is less fun when hopes have been senselessly inflated, or when fine possibilities are bungled by lack of thought and inspiration. Even if a mismanaged occasion may sometimes be enjoyed, the only cardinal error for which one will not be thanked, except in formal expressions, is when one's guests have been led to expect too much. There is nothing more ludicrous than having a loader standing behind one all day when it is abundantly clear that he is redundant. The wise host underestimates the potentiality and allows a generous margin for pleasurable surprise. If a guest is obliged to borrow cartridges before the day is done he will not go home disappointed.

Anticipation played a most delightful part in the King's shooting life. He had the capacity of a young boy for looking forward to the morrow's sport, whether it might be a rough walk or a day of organised driving. But whereas his experience was enriched by numerous disappointments under the category which can be tolerated, mercifully he had relatively few days which were bungled by mismanagement or when his expectations had been senselessly inflated. Most of his shooting was over ground which he knew intimately, and because of the profound interest he took in all developments from month to month he knew fairly accurately what to expect. Though the baffling uncertainties of wild creatures and weather were always liable to be in evidence, His Majesty did not often have occasion to feel thoroughly vexed and exasperated by events.

There was one splendid occasion, however, when, even on his own ground, his expectations and those of his keepers and staff were far exceeded—so much so that the preparations and arrangements were quite unequal to the possibilities, and this particular aspect makes the record quite outstanding.

A certain week of partridge driving which the King organised at very short notice is a record in itself which will probably forever remain unchallenged. In the dark days of the war in 1941 His Majesty was constantly on duty in London or on tour carrying out civil and military duties, and the meagreness of entries in his game book over these several years testifies how few and far between were his days of leave. In the autumn of 1941, however, he was pressed to take a few days off, and went straight to Sandringham. A party was summoned by telephone at twenty-four hours' notice, and on the night of September 28th the company assembled without any presentiment of what was in store for them. On the six days following, the party picked up over 5,000 partridges. This may sound a phenomenal total, but the wartime circumstances render it a truly remarkable accomplishment. Taking into account these conditions, this heavy bag must have represented only a fraction of the birds on the property during that year.

On shoots such as Sandringham and comparable properties before the war there were usually fourteen drives in a day, probably eight before luncheon and six afterwards. The average on this occasion was only ten drives each day, since there was only a handful of beaters, the usual force being seriously depleted by war service, and the picking-up took much longer than usual as this had to be done largely by the party and the keepers, who in normal conditions would have moved straight on to the next drive. The whole interlude could, in fact, be more easily compared with the present-day organisation on an average shoot, and no particular arrangements were made to secure a heavy total as has been done in the case of more publicised record days. Special transport was not available and no time-saving factors were brought into effect.

SHOOTING AT SANDRINGHAM, 1941

10	pheasants	September 29th. *Shernbourne*
882	partridges	
24	hares	Beaufort, David Lyon, Geordie Herbert, Billy Fellowes,
2	various	R. R. Stanton, Joey L. and myself
918		

17	pheasants	September 30th. *Flitcham*
1,358	partridges	
25	hares	Beaufort, David Lyon, Geordie Herbert, Billy Fellowes,
2	pigeons	J. A. Keith, Joey L. and myself
1,402		

21	pheasants	October 1st. *Ling House and Dersingham*
973	partridges	
30	hares	Beaufort, David Lyon, Geordie Herbert, Billy Fellowes,
17	pigeons	O. Birkbeck, Joey L. and myself
1,041		

27	pheasants	October 2nd. *Harpley Dams*
600	partridges	
9	hares	Beaufort, David Lyon, Geordie Herbert, Billy Fellowes,
1	rabbit	J. Holland-Hibbert, Joey L. and myself
6	pigeons	
643		

39	pheasants	October 3rd. *Appleton*
786	partridges	
16	hares	Beaufort, David Lyon, Geordie Herbert, Billy Fellowes,
22	pigeons	S. H. Van Neck, Joey L. and myself
863		

25	pheasants	October 4th. *Ling House* and *Dersingham*
614	partridges	
20	hares	Six guns only
5	pigeons	
664		

Because of the nature of this achievement, without preparations and on a stringent wartime footing, the King always remained very pleased about this particular holiday. He was also very keen on the accuracy of records, and only the year before his death he remarked that it was high time that Gladstone's work on shooting records was brought up to date, having in mind, of course, the absence from this treatise of his own week's partridge total in 1941.

In the annals of partridge shooting there is only one record to compare with this, and that was the bag secured during four days at Holkham in 1905. Holkham only just failed to achieve in four days what Sandringham did in six, but the tremendous differences in circumstances must be taken into account. Indeed, the earlier era was so different from the later, that comparison can hardly be made at all. Nevertheless the two records will forever brighten

---

SHOOTING AT HOLKHAM, 1905

November 7th. *North Point, Warham*

1,671	partridges
10	pheasants
26	hares
2	rabbits
4	golden plover

1,713

November 8th. *Quarles* and *Egmere*

1,030	partridges
30	pheasants
40	hares
3	rabbits

1,103

November 9th. *Wighton*

1,294	partridges
8	pheasants
21	hares
1	rabbit

1,324

November 10th. *Branthill* and *Crabb*

754	partridges
29	pheasants
36	hares
2	rabbits

821

Party.   Prince Frederick Duleep Singh, Mr. W. Barry, Major the Hon. Charles Willoughby, Colonel Custance, Major A. Hood, Mr. W. Forbes, Colonel the Hon. W. Coke, Lord Coke

the pages of shooting history, and permit the student of this art to derive whatever conclusions may please him.

King George the Sixth held no records for a single day, except in the case of a morning duck flight. This is typical of the whole pattern of his shooting life, and is an aspect of which he would have been justly proud.

It may seem somewhat undignified to descend from the realm of game birds and wild duck to coots, but if we have under review less conventional occasions entered in the royal game book, we should perhaps not overlook this item.

A coot on a village pond or garden lake is, at a casual glance, an uninspiring personality. In the select company of various duck species it presents a *bourgeois* appearance and would clearly not be welcomed in the best amphibious circles. Its undistinguished vocal expression, which can only be described as 'click', has a cockney ring about it, and its entire demeanour suggests such unworthy characteristics as clumsiness, lack of breeding, and an irresistible tendency to put its foot in it. The carriage of the coot in the water is a melancholy demonstration of cringing servility; it is unable apparently to swim without a continuous twitching of the neck muscles. On foot it progresses with the utmost indecision, hunched up and with a haunted look, expecting at every step to tread on a landmine. And on a slippery surface there is grotesque humiliation; Norman Wisdom has much to learn from coots on ice.

But this is the coot most commonly recognised, singly or in small numbers, in enclosed places. There is another coot, however, in great quantity on wide expanses of water such as Broadland, and here is a different creature. In winter, especially in hard weather, coots congregate in thousands, and become accustomed, because of the considerable elbow-room and the distances to be traversed, to using their wings. And in flight, with a breeze to help them and uninterrupted flying space at their disposal, they can soar aloft on fluttering pinions into the upper shooting altitudes, and perform in a manner fit to baffle the most erudite performers with a gun. For they not only advance like their more elegant feathered friends but, dependent on the direction of the wind and its strength, frequently go into reverse or fly sideways and indulge in numerous other puzzling manoeuvres. Clearly there is scope here for a diversion in the shooting year, and long ago the coot shoot on Hickling Broad became a traditional round-up at the end of the Norfolk season.

It is the happy tradition of the Hickling circle to consider that this fixture is the only coot shoot ever heard of. But in the past, a similar manoeuvre has in fact yielded considerable bags elsewhere, and referring once more to our friend Payne-Gallwey, we find that he knew as much about it as anyone. 'I have had fine sport with the coots, by driving them slowly from the centre of a lake to one of its ends, by means of a line of boats (each boat containing a shooter). When at length the coots have swum forward till they find themselves cornered, they rise and fly, a few at a time, at a great pace, high overhead, back to the open water. These tactics can sometimes be repeated for the best part of a day, until the coots either leave for other resorts or learn the wisdom of avoiding the boats. In this manner 1,700 coots were, a few years since, killed in one day, to my knowledge, on a large lake in the south of England.' This particular bag exceeds anything ever secured at Hickling.

That coots can provide entertainment for expert sportsmen is testified by the King, who wrote after his first shoot, 'I am so glad to have seen and taken part in the famous Hickling coot shoot. As a day it must be quite unique, and the keepers despite the bad weather did most certainly put the birds over our heads. I did so enjoy the day and I feel I have learnt a lot about coots and their strange flight!'

There was more, however, than just the coots themselves which afforded the King a day which he always enjoyed. In the first place the whole atmosphere of this end-of-season maraud is conducive to festive and at times flippant entertainment. After a season of conventional sport the coot shoot constitutes an engagement of diverting contrast. On this day fifteen friends or more, instead of six or seven, are assembled for the fray. These friends are pushed in Norfolk punts by boatmen, who themselves are traditional figures and as much an integral feature of the scene as the reeds and the bracing air. As well there are the keepers in command and the pickers-up in dinghies, and so there are some forty Norfolk characters assembled to see the shooting season out, an harmonious company well known to each other, a merry band intent, each one in his own capacity, on a successful day. No man of rustic tastes can fail to find entertainment on such an occasion, for if variety is the essence of sport it is surely to be found here. Instead of sitting on a shooting-stick, you sit in a punt. That in itself is a novelty. Instead of swinging on to your bird from two feet planted firmly on terra firma, you swing or roll with the boat, according to the choppiness of the Broad's surface. And instead of being able to observe the performance only of your nearest neighbours in the line, as at a covert shoot, you may scrutinise closely, across the uninterrupted surface of the water, the successes or failures of every member of the party, and because of the 'strange flight' of the coot this facility provokes considerable interest and often jocular comment.

The Hickling coot shoot then is an occasion of high spirits and peculiarly Norfolk sentiment, and as such it had much appeal for His Majesty. The more humorous aspects of his sport were of vast appeal to the King, and the unusual features were subjected to merciless exaggeration, of which Her Majesty the Queen Mother provided evidence when she remarked, after being told later in the year that there had been eighteen guns at a coot shoot, 'Is that all? I understood there were eighty!' On these Hickling days the King had the company of many of his regular winter companions with the gun, and the rest of the assembly was composed of men, both boatmen and sportsmen, of a type with which he was closely familiar. For him it was a proper holiday, a real day out.

The shoot is, however, vulnerable in several respects by reason of the fact that the performers are afloat rather than on foot. You cannot, for example, impel a punt through thick ice, and it is not infrequent to experience a cold snap towards the end of January and to have to cancel the entire performance at short notice.

Again you may walk or stagger forwards in a gale, but a series of punts cannot keep in line in such conditions. Indeed in a hurricane, when the surface of the Broad is whipped into a turbulent fury, the most expert wizardry of the *élite* among Broadland 'pushers' can do no more than maintain a punt in a stationary position and resist a disheartening drift backwards.

And again there are good and bad conditions for driving the coots. In mild weather, when the day is still, a great proportion of the birds make into the reed-beds and disappear. Those that take to the air do so unwillingly and fly poorly, presenting targets without challenge. Or in a high gale disadvantage lies not only with the fleet, for the coots when they rise into the gale give up the unequal struggle very shortly and are blown in uncontrolled confusion round the flanks, over the fields and meadows which lie behind the reed-beds.

Thus every year, though the birds may unquestionably be present, there is some anxiety regarding the weather conditions. The ideal requirements are a fine day with a keen frost, which keeps the coots out of the reeds, and a stiff breeze which brings out the best in their aerial accomplishment.

When it was known that the King would honour Hickling by his participation in a coot shoot, there was always fervent hope for the appropriate meteorological favours. But one year the weather man, with his accustomed animosity towards wildfowlers, was resolved to ensure that all adverse forces should be mobilised to disrupt the enemy's plan. When every detail at Hickling had been worked out with zealous care, the weather man gave the 'go ahead' signal to adverse element Number One and the Broad became frozen over. A melancholy voice called Sandringham by telephone and the date was postponed for two weeks.

The frost was short-lived and all seemed set fair for the revised date. On D-day minus-one some 3,000 coots were massed about the Broad in congested parties, jet-black ranks riding on the ripples, and although there was a strong west wind it seemed that this time there could be no disagreeable turn of events. The party staying in the lodge, however, were startled to awaken on D-day to the sound of wind-torn reeds and rattling windows. A wind of gale force, which was showing no tendency of backing towards fresh or moderate, was lashing the channel beyond the lawn, and on the Broad proper there were white breakers foaming on the leaden grey waters. The weather man was at it again.

Nothing could be done at this stage, for guests would already be on the way, the pushers were assembling, and the King had made an early start from Sandringham. The best would therefore have to made of it.

The previous days of westerly winds had raised the level of the water in the Broad considerably and much of the lawn outside the lodge was flooded. There was a good deal of water on the drive, and the King was much entertained at being required to step from his car in his waders. Frankly, conditions from all aspects could hardly have been worse; the house was all but flooded, the gale precluded any successful manoeuvre in punts, and it was bitterly cold as well. There were serious doubts as to the wisdom of proceeding, and a good deal of despondency pervaded the scene before his arrival.

However, any dismay or faint spirits were entirely dispelled the moment he had stepped from his car with a splash into the gust-torn floodwater that lay everywhere. A chuckle of laughter which escaped him as he decided to pull his waders up to full length relieved the misgivings of the party and set the tone for the performance. He buttoned up his Norfolk jacket round the neck, threw a tweed cape about his shoulders, and splashed his way over to the motor-boat, for the management refused in such an angry sea to commit him to a punt. This craft, in fact, proved most valuable, since time was saved at the outset by taking in tow numerous punts faced with an almost impossible task against the unyielding tempest. The armada advanced resolutely but slowly amidst showers of spray, the sailor King, seated on the box of the motor, at the head of a strange convoy.

In ideal circumstances the various craft move off from the lodge independently and then, as the channel widens towards the Broad itself, which at one point is a mile across, fan out to form a line as if the Broad was to be 'walked up'. It is the Payne-Gallwey drill all over again. As the line advances, the coots in numerous parties, large and small, keep well ahead until, as the party approaches the far end, a vast carpet of coots and fowl of many varieties is concentrated in an area of about half a mile square. The flanks of the line then press forward to form a half-moon, and it is always a source of relief if this somewhat delicate tactical situation is reached without a break by the coots prematurely to a flank, or through some accidental gap in the line.

On the tempestuous occasion which concerns us, however, no well-timed drill was possible. The intention was to tow guns and pushers along the upwind flank of the Broad, and then to peel them off at intervals in the hope that they might be able to half-drift, half-push across the wind and thus seal off the coots in the final position by a different approach. It may sound comparatively simple, but on a tossing sea, in a gale which made all vocal exchange quite inaudible, and with the horizon and neighbouring punts blotted out at intervals by showers of hail and flying spray, it was a miracle that no one was lost. David Bowes-Lyon claims to have come very near to it, according to his own account; the punt seemed suddenly to get a 'roll on' and, despite the efforts of the man with the quant, never came under complete control again, drifting across the swell until it became lodged in the reed-beds some hundreds of yards behind the line. Another guest, who to help matters had gone ahead before the King's arrival and by slow and deliberate work reached a point well up the Broad, was dismayed to see his pilot lose control at the very moment that the King came within earshot of him. With commendable decorum he had decided to get to his feet in order to remove his hat, despite the vigorous movement of the boat, but soon sank wisely to his knees as his boat drifted sickeningly downwind straight for the royal barge and the rest of the armada. This particular participant's presentation consisted of an unwelcome bumping, lurching and spraying for all concerned, whilst the hat bobbed ignominiously away over the waves.

Before long, however, all the punts had been brought into the scene of operations, and discarded in turn to their fate. Finally His Majesty was alone in the motor-boat and all set for the coots on the left of the line, with the remainder, as far as they were able, closing in to his right.

The next development on a day when conditions favour the event is that coots start to rise either across or away from the boats, and when they have reached a proper height, to pass back over the line in an unbroken stream. This may go on for ten or fifteen minutes while the boats traverse the last few hundred yards, and during this phase the fusillade which ensues, of an intensity and volume rarely heard elsewhere in the shooting field, is mindful of a fierce wartime engagement erupting in the forward line. Possibly a thousand cartridges are fired during this first movement in fewer seconds.

But on the King's day there was no such orderly pattern. It was, however, a heartening sight to see him in the thick of the shooting and contending with the situation with such evident relish. The cold, the wet and the turbulence could do nothing to diminish his enjoyment of this unfamiliar scene, and like all good shots he was always intrigued by the coots' flight. He was shooting beautifully, and early on scored a few majestic successes, but as with all other experts there were occasional 'air-shots' with both barrels at what appeared to be comparatively simple targets.

Though puzzling at first, and often disconcerting for the performer, the explanation of these 'inexplicable misses' is simple enough. Shooting on foot one is able to judge the direction and pace of a bird in relation to oneself, knowing, because one's feet are firmly set in the soil, that one is stationary oneself. But in a punt you sit down and look upwards at the birds in the sky. Thus you have no idea in the first place whether the punt is moving or not. Even if it is stationary there is bound to be movement of the boat from side to side, since it tilts whenever the pusher moves or whenever a ripple hits it. This explains probably why the 'easy bird' tends to be missed, the coot which hangs above the boat apparently stationary for some moments. In truth, though the marksman does not know it, his barrels are swinging through the target from side to side like an inverted pendulum, and unless he is fortunate enough to touch off the charge at the precise moment when barrels and bird are in line his shot will go astray. The more impressive bird therefore, high in the air, which requires a quick neat swing, and others which call only for a snap shot, are more frequently brought down than the hovering variety.

A motor-boat rolls less than a punt, however, and despite the heavy 'sea' His Majesty was securely sited for his first innings. The great majority of the coots were riding the waves in the shelter of the western reed-bed and the decision to put the King on the left of the line was proved appropriate. Nearly a hundred coots fell to his gun in only a few minutes. At the far end of the Broad the punts, which by now had given up all hope of keeping in any sort of formation, turned about and made for the southern shore of the Broad, where it is possible to have a coot drive from a deep bay over static positions. Such a manoeuvre had more chance of success on a day of storm and tempest, though if success on this occasion was to be measured only by the degree of enthusiasm demonstrated by the King, no one had any worries from the outset.

That evening a boatman made a picturesque observation which, had it not occurred in Norfolk, would more probably be attributed to an earlier dynasty than to the reign of King George the Sixth. He described how he himself, standing up in the motor-boat, could see five men boat-building beyond the reed-beds, and since the King shot many low coots in that direction, he endeavoured many times to warn him. But the noise and the excitement de-

---

February 11th, 1950   HICKLING BROAD   Coot shoot

457   coots

A. Buxton, David L., Leicester, Somerleyton, C. Mills, K. Watt, R. Cobbold, G. Akroyd, General McHardy, Capt. Dixon, M. Perrin, M. and C. Boardman and myself S.W. gale—most unsuitable weather. Coot very difficult to shoot from a boat.

feated this worthy, and the King continued to bombard the coots. 'In the end,' exclaimed the man, 'I gave it up. After all, if the King shoots a man that don't make a mite o' difference!'

The scene during the next drive presented a dramatic and unforgettable picture. After a violent squall of sleet and hail the storm had blown eastwards and shafts of sunlight pierced the scurrying cloud-masses and defined sunlit areas of striking beauty amidst the darkened landscape. Reed-beds were a shimmering russet and gold, as if a fire glowed within them, whereas in heavy shadow they were sepia. The restless waters, in shadow a leaden grey, suddenly sparkled in the sunlight into the deepest royal-blue, flecked with dancing silver. Every bird, from swan to teal, seemed to be catapulted across a sky of rich deep colours and undisguised fury. The coots, ingeniously driven across the gale, filled the sky like wind-tossed leaves over the centre butts.

And once again, to lend a vivid touch to a Norfolk landscape, in the centre of this bold canvas was His Majesty the King in a reed and timber butt which stands on four stilts out in the Broad; and a King, in a classical wildfowl setting to which he truly belonged, as content as anything in this world could make him. Over a hundred coots were picked up in the vicinity of his butt, shots which ranged from low scuttlers to inspiring downwind gallery shots and crossers well out to a flank. Boatmen and some of the guns were content to stand and watch. If a handful of incidents were to be selected as exceptional moments in the life of a shooting sovereign, this would certainly have been one of them.

The most Spartan fenman could not have failed to welcome the crackling fires and the well-earned sustenance in the lodge which followed. Such weather conditions are exacting, and if it is cold anywhere it is yet colder sitting in an open boat with no freedom to move about or to stamp one's feet. In fact it seemed to be generally assumed among the party that there would be no question of going out again into the hurricane, and that all should be thankful that any sort of sport had been possible on such a day and that the King had had a fair shoot.

Towards the end of luncheon, however, certain observations

made by His Majesty, and finally a request that Piggin, the head keeper,[1] should be brought in to discuss further adventures, made it quite clear to all that there was to be no question of staying indoors; indeed the possibility of not continuing the shoot was never even mentioned. Probably it had never occurred to the King, and was simply wishful thinking on the part of many frozen participants anxious to make His Majesty's comfort an excuse for their failing spirits. However, shelter from the wind, warm fires and certain forms of refreshment do much to fortify failing spirits, and there was general enthusiasm for the resumption of the battle with the elements once it was clear enough that there was to be no escape. The King was soon outside again pulling up his waders, and with little pause had re-embarked in the motor-boat and was away once more towards the Broad.

In the following year entirely different conditions awaited the King. If it is possible to conceive the exact opposite of that stormy day, this was it. The day was so warm that many pushers removed their jackets. The sunshine was so generous that it might have been September or October. And even the most venerable and experienced of ancient coot shooters present could not remember the surface of the Broad being so totally calm in January. There was literally not one tremor, nor a tremble, over all those three hundred acres, and the reflections of the reeds and the birds, of men and punts, were clear and beautiful in the limpid waters.

[1] E. Piggin succeeded Jim Vincent on the death of the latter in 1945.

Janaury 27th, 1951   HICKLING   *The Broad*

4	wild duck	A. Buxton, David L., Leicester, H. Cator, S. Combe,
1	teal	Kimberley, W. Fellowes, C. McLean, O. Birkbeck, K.
9	tufted duck	Watt, M. Perrin, Col. Blacker, Brig. Clewes, Capt.
3	pochard	Dixon, C. and M. Boardman, W. Aitken and myself
1	golden-eye	
961	coots	A lovely sunny day. Broad very calm with not a ripple on
—		it. The coot did not fly too high, but they came over well.
979		

Such a day however, as already described, is not ideal for this occasion and in general the birds were not shown at their best. Nevertheless it was impossible, in such a joyous winter's setting, to feel any complaint about anything, and it was a vivid pleasure for all simply to sit in a punt on the Broad—which cannot often be said for January. There were duck in quantity of many species flying about all day, and the various drakes were most elegant in the sunlight. It was the happiest of days, with the happiest of company. There were gathered together not only some of His Majesty's lifelong friends, and especially companions of fen and and broad, but also a truly representative team of the Norfolk shooting fraternity. Once more, as had happened at Sandringham on a morning flight, this might have been a set-piece, the whole scene and the arrangement grouped round the person of the wild-fowler King, with wonderful weather to enhance the charm and the magic of Broadland. This was a perfect day and, looking back, how splendid that it was so.

For, as it proved, this was His Majesty's last day in Broadland.

As he stepped from his punt in the afternoon sunshine, after a day of cheerful companionship and vigorous sport, he stepped from a Norfolk punt for the last time. This great sportsman, our King, whose flight-shooting in East Norfolk will become legendary, was making his last round. For in the twenty-four hours beforehand he had been on Ranworth Flood and Cockshoot. Now, for a final day in Broadland company, he was at Hickling.

As his car bore him away along the marshland drive, the King of England saw for the last time reed-beds glowing in the sunset and the horizon mirrored in still waters.

X

THE LAST SEASON

Next autumn the King set off for his usual holiday at Balmoral. But whereas his subjects had always rejoiced to think that he was wrapped up in peaceful seclusion on Deeside with his friends and his gun, during this autumn of 1951 undisguised anxiety, a lurking fear which no man or woman could conceal, gripped the nation's heart. His Majesty was seriously ill.

The calm and noble dignity of this sick man flying south for a day to visit a London specialist brought a lump to many throats. Here was courage to inspire, a brave example to spread comfort. But nothing could dispel the national sensation of foreboding, and the King's subjects of all ranks, creeds and colour could not be reassured. Unhappily they were right.

Yet it is inspiring now to know that the King never allowed those gathering storm-clouds to dominate his thoughts, nor did he permit the minds of his companions to dwell on them. At Balmoral he was still the same laird, alert to every detail, eager for sporting news, pertinacious and critical. And on that very evening that he landed once again at Dyce Airport, while hearts stood still in fearful speculation at the consequences of that trip, the King, on arrival at Balmoral, went at once to the sand table-model of the moors and forest to hear explained in every detail the experiences of the shooting party which he had been obliged to despatch that day without himself.

One thought gave him much happiness. His own accomplishment as a shot had from the outset fired the enthusiasm of his son-in-law, and with his remarkable gift for learning anything new, Prince Philip, after only a few seasons, acquired a degree of skill in the shooting field which many fail to show after a lifetime of sport. The King taught him not only the rudiments of game shooting, but all the finer methods of pursuit. Like his father-in-law, Prince Philip became a seasoned expert, whether the quarry was a grouse or a partridge, a duck or a coot.

And so the King knew that future generations could enjoy all that he had created, and that through his example the same spirit and understanding would be applied.

Royal shooting ceased on September 14th, and there followed a pause in the sequence of game-book entries. Some time later he wrote in the book, 'I did not shoot in October, November or December because of my lung operation.'

These are not the pages in which to dwell on such anxious moments and painful memories. The dread day passed, the operation was successfully performed, and the peoples of the Commonwealth gradually dared to breathe again as His Majesty first came through the great danger, and then steadily recovered his strength. When he first rose from his bed he was keen to discover if his arms would lift easily above the shoulder, and playfully he raised them two or three times as if bringing a gun to his shoulder. Though the act was half in fun, there was a twinkle of merriment in His Majesty's eyes when he realised he might still be able to enjoy his favourite pastime.

The long days of autumn passed, whilst his own people in Norfolk waited in hopeful expectation of his return. Towards Christmas the King came home, and to a friend he wrote, 'I am so pleased to be back in Norfolk once more.' Then, quietly, Sandringham life was resumed, the shadow of the dark days passed, and this particular family interlude, the royal Christmas in Norfolk, assumed once more its precious and traditional character.

August 21st, 1951 BALMORAL *Tomboddies* and *Blairglass*

1	hare	Philip, Salisbury, Eldon, Dalkeith, R. McEwen, Althorp
3 (1)	snipe	and myself
300	grouse	

——

304	Fine. Cold W. wind. Some young birds not fully grown.

There were some small days in the woodlands, good sporting occasions conforming to the post-war pattern, a hundred pheasants or so and a few oddments thrown in. The King was under careful medical care, and things were taken easy. The days were shortened, and he always moved about in his Land-rover.

At the close of each season the Sandringham shooting did not cease abruptly, but parties continued to assemble for a few informal fixtures in February, before His Majesty returned to London and the keepers to their separate beats for the spring and summer tour of duty. This last phase included afternoons flighting pigeons, days after rabbits in the coverts, and large parties deployed across the landscape driving hares.

Like every good shot, the King thoroughly enjoyed a pigeon flight. His pigeon-shooting, however, conformed with modest standards and he never in all his shooting days experienced anything exceptional or a flight comparable with the more notable pigeon shoots in the country. Success with pigeons depends, in the first place, on what birds are available in the area, and secondly, on how extensive or how restricted are the roosting-places.

The famous Cambridgeshire pigeon woods, for example, lie in the heart of a great expanse of feeding-grounds, where pigeon congregate in the winter and early spring in their thousands. The woodlands are widely scattered, and often separated by a mile or more, and the roosting accommodation is therefore limited. Thus all suitable woods are in great demand at roosting time, and during a shoot, when most coverts are occupied by guns, the pigeons often surge in droves from one roosting-place to the next.

September 5th, 1951 BALMORAL *Glaschville*
  1 rabbit   Philip, David L., John E., M. Sinclair, M. Adeane,
  1 black game Plunket and myself
322 grouse
———   Fine and sunny. S.W. wind. Saw a nice few birds all day.
324

Sandringham, on the other hand, is neither one thing nor the other. There is good feeding for pigeons in the heart of Norfolk farmland, but Sandringham itself is very wooded and the roosting opportunities are considerable. There is no adequate concentration of pigeons therefore to afford a single shooter an impressive bag.

Nevertheless during his reign His Majesty always went out on a few occasions during January and February. Tenant farmers, neighbours and keepers all took part, and were dispersed on an appointed afternoon about the estate. Usually there were anything up to a dozen guns, and an average of ten pigeons to a gun was fair for the estate, and often the bag was less. But pigeons are such superb sport, in that they put to the test every man's shooting prowess to a greater degree than any other game or wildfowl, that there is always the incentive to go out again. The fascination of pigeons lies in their astonishing powers of manoeuvre and in their marvellous sight.

Looking at random through the King's game book we find that on February 8th, 1951, six guns picked up 51 pigeons. The King notes that the pigeons were 'chary of coming in to roost', and since the weather was 'fine' this is readily appreciated. Fine and sunny weather is almost hopeless. A week later eight guns killed 93 pigeons, and one may quote a host of such days, with the bag fluctuating over or under ten birds per gun.

The King only once got a good bag of pigeons by Cambridgeshire standards, and that was before the war, in 1930 at Massingham, not far from Sandringham. In a south-westerly gale four

---

September 14th, 1951   BALMORAL   *Caloke Corrie* and *Dalnabo*

38 hares	Harry, Philip, David L., John E., Porchester, E. Heywood-Lonsdale and myself
1 pigeon	
302 grouse	
————	Fine. A strong S.W. wind made things difficult.
341	

(His Majesty's last day shooting in Scotland.)

guns got 57 pigeons, but of this total His Majesty got 40 himself. Forty is a good personal score, for an evening's bag is usually secured in an hour or two and the sport is constant and exciting.

But apart from this occasion His Majesty's pigeon-shooting was a modest business, and it would be senseless to make out that it was anything else. Nevertheless it is significant that this shooting King, who enjoyed the cream of sport at game and wildfowl, was still ready to wait out in winter weather for a dozen pigeons or less.

The other method of shooting pigeons, apart from flighting or intercepting them by accident on migration (and from the game book it does not appear that His Majesty ever struck this rare chance), is to wait for them on the feeding-grounds. In hard weather, and particularly in snow, it is well worth waiting in green crops. The King tried this medium on several occasions, and with evident relish on the day already quoted, when he spent 'four hours in a hide in a kale field'. On this occasion three guns collected 94 pigeons, of which the King picked up 43.

At the same time of the year, when he was able to linger on for a few February days at Sandringham, rabbit or hare shoots took place almost every day. These events were arranged in a manner that is the custom on all large properties, the host assembling with his agent and tenants, whilst the head keeper mobilises the small farmers, the police and other local personalities. There may be a score of guns or more, and most days afford a welcome opportunity for all factions of the local community to spend a day to-

---

January 1st, 1952 SANDRINGHAM *Heath Farm*
101 pheasants Philip, Dalkeith, E. Bacon, G. Gordon-Lennox, Tryon,
  4 hares M. Adeane and myself
 11 rabbits
  4 woodcock Fine and cold. Birds flew well. Cocks only.
  1 pigeon

121

BALMORAL
The King with his dog "Glen"

gether. His Majesty particularly enjoyed a day out with his neighbours from all walks of life.

The royal family had never taken part in these tail-end pursuits before the King discovered that they were very much to his liking. He did not, in fact, make this discovery until towards the end of his life, but in the last few years, when hare and rabbit shooting became a serious business, he not only derived unusual enthusiasm from what is to many men only moderate entertainment, but developed, at rabbits in particular, the most exceptional skill. At rabbits he was in a class by himself.

Hares were shot in the approved style, by driving them in a vast sweep towards a line of guns who sat on the forward side of a hedge. His Majesty used to sit forward all day, and once again was exceptionally accurate. One thing that always impressed the experienced observer was the fact that he was so deadly at awkward and unpopular shots. The best performers often miss hares, even close by and moving slowly. Similarly the best shots in the land often fail to kill cleanly a pheasant which rises ponderously at the feet and flies straight away, presenting a large rear view to the marksman. But at these unsatisfying targets the King was extraordinarily consistent, and hares, like rabbits, stood little chance of escape if they ventured within range of his gun. The true reason for all this proficiency lay in the King's intense powers of concentration. When a great big fat pheasant rises in front of us we probably do not try because it looks so easy. So with a lolloping hare. But the King, like a first-class cricketer, watched every ball, and his style and technique were never permitted to deteriorate or become slack.

It was in the enjoyment of such informal days after hares, rabbits, and pigeons, in the midst of his Sandringham company, that His Majesty passed his last weeks. And it was on such a day after hares that he spent his last day in the open.[1]

[1] The bag on this last day's shooting, which was not entered in the game book, was 280 hares, 4 rabbits and 2 pigeons. There were some twenty guns in the party, including tenants, the police and visiting gamekeepers. His Majesty got 9 hares at the last stand and 3 with his last three shots.

The Norfolk scene was set for the occasion, the wide arc of blue sky, sunshine and long shadows, a crispness underfoot and the call of mating partridges ringing clearly across broad fields.

They were all there, the King's men—his staff, some friends, the keepers, the estate workers, and all. The day went well, and the host enjoyed it.

For the last drive the King sat waiting on the forward bank of the hedge, and another hedge to his flank stretched forward at right angles to the line of guns, between himself and the next gun. Before the drive began, he merrily chided his neighbour, one who had spent as much time with him at Sandringham as anyone, 'I bet I shoot any hares before they cross that hedge to you!'

A great many hares came forward that drive. Towards the end they seemed to see the King and darted through the hedge towards his neighbour. The first was bowled over by His Majesty on the crest of the bank. His friend looked across and was greeted with a gleeful grin. The second was far out in front when it made the hedge, but the King got it none the less. The third, and the last, was at full speed, for the drivers were close in, but His Majesty killed it cleanly against the hedge.

It was his last shot.

. . . . . .

How vastly different was this sport from the fixtures of previous reigns! In these few pages we have traced a strange course, where royal bags fell from four figures to three, two and often to one,

---

January 24th, 1952 SANDRINGHAM *Church Farm* and *Eleven Acres*

90	pheasants	Philip, Leicester, Euston, C. Smith-Ryland, Mr. W. P.
12	hares	Thompson, Tryon and myself
5	rabbits	
2	pigeons	Fine but cold and still. Cocks only.
3	various	
112		

but where skill, knowledge and sportsmanship emerged from a background of conventional parade-ground bombardment. King George the Sixth was at the forefront of this great awakening; he was foremost among the new artists of the chase, and above all, if his lessons are studied, he has shown shooting men how their pursuit should be conducted, without cruelty and without abuse.

.   .   .   .   .   .

At dawn on the following day there was silence in Norfolk. Soon all the country was hushed. By a cause unrelated to his recent illness, the King had died in the night.

And as he was carried from his house to the little church, where his gamekeepers were to stand guard over him, they say a cock pheasant crowed in the parkland.

INDEX TO NAMES ENTERED
IN THE GAME BOOK

Uncle Alge — Earl of Athlone

Uncle Charles — King Haakon VII of Norway

David — H.R.H. the Duke of Windsor

David Lyon, David L. — The Honourable David Bowes-Lyon

Harold C. — Commander Sir Harold Campbell

Harry — H.R.H. the Duke of Gloucester

Joey L. — Colonel the Honourable Sir Piers Legh

John E. — The Master of Elphinstone

Lilibet — Her Majesty Queen Elizabeth II

Michael Lyon, Michael L. — Colonel the Honourable Michael Bowes-Lyon

Papa — His Majesty King George the Fifth

Philip — H.R.H. the Duke of Edinburgh

Sidney E. — Lord Elphinstone